THE REVELATION AND THE RAPTURE —

ARE WE THERE YET?

"See to it that no one misleads you. For many will come in My name...
and will deceive many...if possible even the elect."
Matthew 24:4,5 & 24

A Study of
The Basics of Biblical Eschatology

By

ROBERT L. KRAMER

Copyright © 2007 by Robert L. Kramer

*THE REVELATION AND THE RAPTURE—
ARE WE THERE YET?*
by Robert L. Kramer

Printed in the United States of America

ISBN-13: 978-1-60034-857-0
IBSN-10: 1-60034-857-2

All rights reserved solely by the author. The author guarantees all contents are original and do not infringe upon the legal rights of any other person or work. No part of this book may be reproduced in any form without the permission of the author. The views expressed in this book are not necessarily those of the publisher.

Scripture quotations are from the New American Standard Bible, Copyright © 1900, 1962, 1963, 1968, 1971, 1972, 1973, 1975, 1977 by the Lockman Foundation.

www.xulonpress.com

DEDICATED

To God's gifts to me – my wife, Evelyn Weaver Kramer, housewife, typist, proof-reader and friend and helper to all – and to our five most wonderful God-loving children of whom we are justly proud and whom we dearly love, Joyce A. Trievel, Dale A. Kramer, Faye K. Price, Bruce L. Kramer, and Jayne L. Hontz.

CONTENTS

Forward ix
Preface xi
Introduction xv

UNIT ONE: DECEPTION ABOUT THE FUTURE 19

Chapter 1:   Exploring the Problem 21
Chapter 2:   Jesus Forewarns of Deception 29
Chapter 3:   The Great Tribulation of Israel 37
Chapter 4:   The Great Tribulation of the Church 49
Chapter 5:   The Revelation of Christ and
             the Rapture 57
Chapter 6:   A Comprehensive Chronological Outline
             of the Future 71

UNIT TWO: CLARIFYING ESCHATOLOGICAL
           TEXTS 91

Chapter 7:   The Time Frame of Daniel's Prophecies 93
Chapter 8:   The Time Frame of Ezekiel's
             Prophecies 115

Chapter 9: The Church in the Revelation..................127
Chapter 10: I Will Come Again—John 14:1-3................145

UNIT THREE: CLARIFYING ESCHATOLOGICAL ISSUES...................157

Chapter 11: Will Christians Go Through the Tribulation or the Day of Wrath?..................159
Chapter 12: Vultures and Eagles..................167
Chapter 13: What Jesus Taught About the Future of Israel..................175
Chapter 14: The Destiny of Unrepentant Sinners: Eternal Torture or Eternal Death..................199
Chapter 15: An Open Letter to Any and All Pretribulationalists..................215

ADDENDUM: The Purpose of Prophecy..................231

FORWARD

—⟿—

Robert Kramer has written a remarkable book. The sub title "A Study of the Basics of Biblical Eschatology" goes to the heart of the author's theological concepts.

One may not agree with every viewpoint that Kramer shares in the book that embraces a life-time of study and prayer; but he will find this book easy to read, enlightening and saturated with biblical truth.

The conclusions that Kramer draws in his end-time teachings are quite formidable. Every reader will have a greatly expanded understanding of the Bible's forecast of the future and certainly gain many fresh insights into the return of Christ and related events when he reads this monumental work.

        Preston A. Taylor
        Pastor, Trinity Baptist Church
        Miranda City, Texas
        Author, "The Thirteen Apostles"
        "Jesus: King of Kings" (The Revelation)

PREFACE

Every writer and teacher of Biblical eschatology and everyone who reads what they write and hears what they teach needs to subscribe to two important truths in order to maintain a proper perspective toward the subject and those who teach it.

Number 1: A Knowledge of the Future Is Not Necessary for Personal Salvation

Our personal salvation does not depend on one having a perfect or a particular viewpoint about the future.

It is our understanding of and faith in the past activities of God, that is, the incarnation, crucifixion, resurrection and ascension of Christ that will save us; not our understanding of the future, which God will control and bring to pass, as He, in His eternal wisdom, will order it.

Premillennialists, postmillennialists, amillennialists, preterists, historicists, futurists, posttribulationalists, midtribulationalists and pretribulationalists will all go to heaven as the children of God who have confessed their sinfulness and have accepted by faith the atoning merits of the Lord Jesus Christ.

This being the case, we should be able to discuss and explore our different interpretations of Biblical prophecy with much love and respect for each other and with a sincere desire to discover the truth not simply to defend a position. Biblical prophecy is not something to cause one brother to despise and break fellowship with another.

Number 2: No One Has Perfect Understanding Or All the Answers About the Future

Every writer and every teacher of Biblical eschatology must humbly admit that his understanding of it is not perfect or complete. However, while some have merely dabbled in Biblical prophecy as they might pursue a hobby; and some have read a few books and perceived themselves to be expert on the subject or have chosen a favorite author or TV preacher and adopted him as their prophecy guru—others of us have concentrated on a continuing passionate study of the prophetic Scriptures themselves not simply what others in their commentaries have said about them.

For more than 30 years, I have devoted much of my considerable study time to Biblical eschatology; and the time spent in that study and the intensity of it has greatly increased during the last 13 years since my retirement from the pastorate.

Thus, while claiming no perfection or completeness, I have given the Holy Spirit time and opportunity to instruct me in the Word and to fashion an eschatology that makes sense to me and can be defended and supported by ample and contextually correct Scriptural texts.

About thirteen years ago I began writing and mailing a Bible study periodical called Second Thoughts, which focused mainly on prophetic themes. I was partly motivated to begin that ministry by a statement in the foreword of the New International Biblical Commentary which read, "Although exact scholarship has its place in the service of Christ, those who share in the teaching office of the church have a responsibility to make the results of their research accessible to the Christian community at large."

As a pastor and a Bible student, I have not been able to share the attitude expressed by people who minimize Biblical prophecy and consider it too difficult or controversial to pursue. A bishop known for his dry wit once said with tongue in cheek, "I don't get caught up in Biblical prophecy because God's gonna do it His way anyway." Well, that is true, but God has chosen to reveal His intentions for the future. He has given to us some foreknowledge of what is to come in order to encourage, enlighten and motivate us to persevere in the faith until we receive the inheritance He is laying in store for us.

INTRODUCTION

Back to Basics

A number of years ago I was playing one-on-one basketball at our church camp in the Pocono mountains of Pennsylvania against a young staff member half my age and a few inches taller. While trying difficult unorthodox shots which one would not try very often in a normal game I was staying close but not winning. Then I thought to myself, "Enough of this nonsense" and repeatedly said to my opponent, "Ok! It is back to basic shots, only basic shots from now on." I began shooting straight-on jump shots ten to fifteen feet from the basket and hitting enough of them to defeat my younger and taller opponent.

The church has gotten away from the basics of its eschatological doctrine. They have been deceived by well-meaning and sincere evangelically minded men who by their persistent, tireless repetition of unscriptural theories have, in cult like fashion, brainwashed millions into departing from the historical position of the church to accept the sensationalized modern eschatology created by them.

To get back to basics is to return to the posture of the early church and the church fathers who believed in one Second Coming and anticipated the public visible revelation of Jesus not a prior rapture. The late Dr. John Walvoord, former president of Dallas Theological Seminary and a recognized proponent of pretribulationalism, admitted, "Posttribulationalism was the position held by a majority of the early church and is the most widely held interpretation today." In his book <u>The Church In Prophecy</u> he wrote, "The posttribulationalism of our day in some respects corresponds to the view of the early church fathers and in other respects is decidedly different and recent. In the church of the second and third century, it was commonly believed that the church was already in the great tribulation predicted by Christ... Their view of the Lord's return was that it was both post-tribulational and imminent."

Many pretribulationalists, who proudly consider themselves fundamental Bible believing Christians, do not realize or will not admit that they have abandoned the historic New Testament faith and teaching about the future to follow a modernistic eschatological doctrine that has been built upon arbitrary assumptions and traditions developed by men.

What is believed to be the historic belief of the church—that the revelation of Jesus and the accompanying rapture would occur after the tribulation (however that is perceived)—was challenged in the early 1800s when the new theory of pretribulationalism was introduced, bringing with it gross error and confusion that continues today.

The appeal of pretribulationalism is, of course, the promise and prospect of missing the great tribulation, especially when the nature of that event is wrongly perceived as well as its timing.

Built upon a forced and false interpretation of Daniel 9:24-27 pretribulationalists have been duped into believing that there is a gap in the 490 years before the promises of Daniel 9:24 are fulfilled; that the last seven years are yet to come; that the seven last years are the great tribulation; that the prince who is to come is the antichrist and that he is the one who will make a covenant with Israel.

In addition five assumptions are made and taught about the rapture—that the Second Coming is split into two trips; that the rapture is separated from and occurs seven years before the revelation of Christ; that the rapture is secretive and sudden as the blink of an eye and those who are raptured are taken to heaven.

The chief weakness of pretribulationalism is that <u>not one</u> of the above mentioned foundational tenets can be found clearly stated in the Scriptures. They are based on wrong assumptions, suppositions and deductions made from the texts. These things are then taught with such persistence and repetition that its adherents accept its tenets without question or honest searching of the Scriptures to determine if they conform to them. I repeat there is not one verse in the whole Bible that simply and clearly says that any of the foundational tenets as stated above are true. That is scary; and it is pitiful that so many have been persuaded to believe that these assumptions are true. One would think—and hope—that an intelligent person who is eager to know the truth of God's word would step back and take another honest look at what he has been taught and now believes. It is my purpose in writing the following chapters to give the reader an opportunity to do just that.

Doctrinal Divisions

To understand how widespread is the confusion and deception about the future within the ranks of Christianity we need only to contemplate the fact that we are divided into premillennial, postmillennial and amillenial camps. In addition, there are pretribulationalists, midtribulationalists and posttribulationalists. There are those who interpret Biblical eschatology from a preterist, historicist, futurist and an idealist persuasion. Plus there are endless varieties of beliefs and teachings within each of these schools of interpretation. These various groups do not represent only minor variations from a commonly held core of truths. They each view the future in ways that are significantly different from the others.

Multitudes Deceived

If any one of these persuasions is a correct interpretation of the future, then all the others must be deceitful and erroneous. Further, I do not believe that any one of these groups and their interpretation of Biblical eschatology is embraced by the majority of Christians. If none of the groups have a majority of Christians in their camp and only one of the groups can be correct in its interpretation of prophecy—then the obvious conclusion must be that *the majority of Christians are being deceived* in what they are taught and believe about the future. This is a matter we all need to be concerned about. It behooves those of us who have the divine call and responsibility to teach and preach the Word of God and the prophecies contained therein to guard against a stubborn and prideful defense of a position or a system rather than honestly searching for the truth no matter where it will take us. We need also to be willing to engage in dialogue with each other as brothers in the hope that we can eventually be led closer to the center and find a truly Spirit inspired understanding of divine truth.

UNIT ONE

DECEPTION ABOUT THE FUTURE

CHAPTER ONE

EXPLORING THE PROBLEM

The prophetic climate in the church was typified by the beautiful young woman who stood before me one day. She was relatively new in the faith, but loyal to her church and eager to grow in her faith and in her knowledge of the Word. Frustration and perplexity were evident by the tension in her voice and the frown on her face as she verbalized what others were feeling but hesitated to express. "Pastor Bob, can you help me? I am totally confused about the future and especially the great tribulation. You have been telling us that the church will go through the tribulation and that it has been going on throughout this age and may intensify before Christ returns and raptures us out of tribulation. That scares me! The preachers I hear on TV and all my friends say that Jesus will secretly return and snatch us up suddenly to take us to heaven while seven years of terrible tribulation take place on earth. I must say, 'that sounds good to me.' Then while I am trying to sort this thing out someone in our Bible study group said that Christians will go through only half of the tribulation until Christ returns to take us to heaven; so we will miss the worst half of the tribulation. I do not know Pastor Bob, what am I to believe? How are we supposed to intelligently and with any confidence look to the future and await the coming of Christ when all these respected and sincere pastors and teachers are telling us such different and conflicting stories?"

This study is an attempt to answer that young lady's question. We encourage the readers to read for themselves each quoted Scriptural text and to prayerfully ask the Spirit to give them understanding of those texts; then accept whatever the Bible simply and plainly says and reject all else even if it is written in this book and by this author. Test all you hear and read by the Word of God.

Today's Confused Prophecy Teachers

Most evangelical Christians are confused or deceived by today's popular prophecy teachers and preachers into believing theories about the future, especially about the rapture and the great tribulation, that are sadly wrong because they cannot be supported by clear simple statements from the Word of God.

Many respected evangelical preachers, authors and prophecy teachers have been saying rather emphatically and repeatedly that we are the last generation, the generation that will witness the Lord's sudden secretive coming for the rapture of the saints.

It was almost a generation ago in 1970 that Dr. Hal Lindsey wrote unequivocally that the present generation is the last (terminal) generation that Jesus talked about in Matthew 24:34. He also taught that 1988 might have been the time of the rapture and the time when "the last great war would be fought that would wipe out nearly all human life off the planet." He further believed and wrote that the return of Christ would probably certainly be before the year 2000. Was Hal Lindsey correct? Obviously not! He had three swings and shamefully struck out.

Dr. Harold Camping, the founder of Family Radio, wrote a thick book explaining and affirming that it would all happen in 1994. Was Dr. Camping correct? Obviously not! He had much to say on the subject of Christ's return but only proved that he knew very little about it.

On September 18, 1993, I heard Dr. Jack VanImpe say in his television program, "The wind up is coming by the year 2000. I will prove that next week." Later in a book written by him, he set the date for September 1999. He also predicted a Russian invasion of the USA to occur in 1996. Was Dr. VanImpe correct in any of these predictions? Obviously not, another strike out, yet he still comes to bat once a week and many loyal spectators still watch him strike out and still send their support to keep him swinging.

The co-author of the Left Behind series of fiction books, Dr. Tim LaHaye, wrote in his 1972 book, <u>The Beginning of the End</u>, about the generation which is supposedly to be raptured, "It is the generation...or the people who saw the first World War." He went on to clarify that they were..."perhaps somewhere between five years and fourteen years of age in 1914. I believe it is that generation which our Lord said, 'will not pass away till all those things...be fulfilled'." Thus, Dr. LaHaye was saying that those born from 1900 to 1909 comprise the generation which would be raptured. Was Dr. LaHaye correct? Obviously not! The great majority of those born from 1900 to 1909 are now deceased. Jesus had not raptured them as Dr. LaHaye surmised. According to Dr. LaHaye's dates, the rapture should have already happened. I guess he and all the rest of us who are still living missed it and were LEFT BEHIND!

John Hagee, a popular radio and TV preacher and author wrote in 1996, "Grasp with your head and heart this overpowering truth from the Word of God—We are the terminal generation!" Is Pastor Hagee correct? We will not know until we are all dead or raptured.

The sad fact is that although the above named and other respected evangelical Christians make prophecies that have been or are being proved wrong, they do not lose any credibility with their followers. Fellow pretribbers continue to eagerly accept every deceptive and presumptive word from their mouths and pens.

These men and others who have set dates—whether their dates were precise as to the month or the year or as broad as naming a particular generation—all have two things in common. #1. All of them were or are pretribulationalists. #2. All of them have been wrong!

The Base of the Deceit & Error: The Rapture & the Tribulation

Everyone's eschatology is shaped not so much by his perception of the timing of the Lord's return to earth as it is by the perceived timing of the rapture in relation to the great tribulation. Pretribbers, midtribbers as well as posttribbers all agree that Jesus' return to earth in order to establish His millennial kingdom will be posttribulational; our differences relate to the timing of the rapture. Therefore, if one's understanding of the timing and nature of the rapture and great tribulation is wrong it is certain that much of his total eschatology will be wrong.

The Christian church is blessed with fine Christian gentlemen like Hal Lindsey, Tim LaHaye, Jack VanImpe, John Hagee, Jerry Falwell and a host of others who are to be respected and admired for the gospel they believe and preach, but Jesus fore-warned that even the elect can be deceived as they try to discern the signs of the times and the prophesied future events.

Contrary to what these men and their fellows believe and teach, as stated earlier, there is not a single verse in the Bible that simply and clearly says that there is a gap in Daniel's 70 weeks (490 years), or an antichrist or a 7 year tribulation.

There is not a single verse in the Bible that simply and clearly says that the second coming of Christ is split into two trips seven years apart and that the rapture will occur seven years before the revelation of Jesus. Nor does the Bible anywhere say that it will be as sudden as the twinkling of an eye or secretive.

There is not a single verse in the Bible that simply and clearly says that raptured Christians will be taken to heaven after meeting the Lord in the air and that they will be gone for 3 1/2 or 7 years. Yet these are the beliefs and teachings of most of the popular prophecy teachers and preachers and their evangelical Christian followers.

I have observed in my reading of hundreds of books by pretribulational proponents that none of them present an exhaustive and convincing body of Scriptural texts to establish the correctness of their understanding of the nature and timing of the great tribulation. It is generally introduced as an established event that needs no Scriptural verification for its validity.

We shall attempt to unravel the confusion about the great tribulation in a subsequent chapter by studying all the texts and the historical background that seem to relate to it with the hope that those who are in a quandary about it, as well as those who may be vainly hanging on to what they wrongly assume to be a correct Biblical viewpoint, may, at least, be open to and challenged to take a second look at this important subject—and, thereby, discover what Jesus actually taught about it.

Two Major Mistakes

There are two major mistakes that are generally made about the great tribulation when taught even by the most popular prophecy teachers.

Failure to Discern Two Lines of Tribulation Related in the Bible

Anytime the words tribulation or great tribulation are used in the Bible, it is easy to wrongly assume that they are always referring to the same event or time period. In a careful and unbiased study of the subject, one discovers that there is not one, but two lines of tribulation announced and traced in the Scriptures.

In the twelfth chapter of the Revelation John was given a flashback vision of the birth (12:1,5) and ascension (12:5) of Jesus and events that immediately followed. This was done to reveal to John the historical circumstances that had brought him and the church into the tribulation in which they found themselves (1:9).

After the ascension of Jesus (12:5) there was a war in heaven which resulted in Satan being cast out of heaven to the earth. He vented his anger on the woman, Israel, (12:13-16) whom he persecuted and then also her offspring, the church of the Lord Jesus (12:17). Thus, the Bible foretells a great tribulation that came upon Israel and a separate outpouring of persecution or great tribulation upon the church.

The words *great tribulation* are found in only three texts in the New Testament—Matthew 24:21-28, Acts 11:19 as it refers back to Acts 8:1 and in Revelation 7:14.

In Matthew 24:21-28 Jesus predicted a soon to come great tribulation of Israel (also Mk. 13:19 and Jer. 30:7). This was to be primarily a local Jewish tribulation, which was fulfilled in AD 67-70. There is nothing in Jesus' words (Mt. 24:21-28) to suggest that this was to be a world-wide tribulation; and nothing that corresponds to what is described in the Revelation chapters 8-19.

Acts 11:19, which reports the stoning of Stephen as originally told in Acts 8:1, refers to the great tribulation of the church, as does Revelation 7:14.

It is important to note that none of these passages in any way suggest that either of these tribulations were limited to a seven year period. They both began after the ascension of Jesus and continue from time to time and place to place throughout this age and will do so until the Lord returns.

Nowhere does the Bible tell of a seven year tribulation period—NOWHERE! The whole erroneous theory of a seven year tribulation is based on an arbitrary misinterpretation of Daniel 9:26-27. It is wrongly taught that there is a gap between the 69th and 70th weeks and that the 70th week of seven years will be a future period of great tribulation. Daniel 9:24-27 says nothing about a gap, the antichrist or a great tribulation still to come. That prophecy was all about the first coming of our Lord, His death and the new covenant He initiated and the subsequent destruction of Jerusalem, which occurred in AD 70. Unfortunately, a whole confusing and deceptive eschatology has been built around an arbitrary and erroneous interpretation of Daniel 9:24-27 and many unquestioningly follow it.

Confusing the Great Tribulation With the Day of Wrath

Many make the mistake of equating the great tribulation with the day of wrath. They are separate periods in human history.

There is a significant difference between tribulation and wrath. The Greek word for tribulation is thlipsis. It is sometimes translated affliction and connotes any sort of heavy external pressure that comes upon the people of God. It comes upon the church from the surrounding unbelieving world and Satanic forces within the world. It is permitted by God, but the source of the tribulation is Satan and the unbelieving world.

On the other hand, the day of wrath is a brief period of time and events which God initiates and actively sends upon the world as judgments for their irreverence and wickedness. His wrath will come in the form of natural or supernatural phenomena upon mankind and his environment.

Jesus foretold that the great tribulation of Israel would begin when His apostles saw the abomination of desolation in the holy place (Mt. 24:15-21) and Jerusalem surrounded by armies (Lk. 21;20); which they saw in AD 67-70.

Luke wrote that the great tribulation of the church began in Jerusalem upon the stoning of Stephen (Ac. 8:1 & 11:19).

While the great tribulation of Israel and the church have both begun nearly 2000 years ago, the day of wrath has not yet come. According to Revelation 6:16-17, the day of wrath will follow this age of great tribulation. The sixth seal signs, which precede and announce the nearness of Christ's return (Rev. 6:12-17), were foretold by Jesus to His disciples as recorded in Matthew 24:29; and He clearly affirmed that they would occur *"after the tribulation."* Therefore, the periods of the trumpets (Rev. 8-9) and of the bowls (Rev. 14-16) cannot be descriptive of the great tribulation. In the Revelation, the seals (6:1-17) cover the period of the great tribulation while the trumpets and the bowls (6:16-19:21) cover the day of wrath as so labeled in 6:17, 11:18, 14:10 & 19, 15:1 and 16:1 & 19.

We hope, in the following chapters, to verify by clear statements from the Scriptures that many of the popular prophecy teachers are teaching gross error and that many—possibly the majority—of Christians, who fervently believe they have the future all figured out, have been deceived by these popular, sincere and well-intentioned teachers.

This should not strike one as unthinkable or surprising since, as we shall present in the next chapter, Jesus foresaw and warned against this possibility.

And since the great tribulation and the rapture are at the center of this deceitful teaching, in subsequent chapters we shall present detailed studies of what the Bible actually teaches on those subjects.

CHAPTER TWO

JESUS FOREWARNS OF DECEPTION ABOUT THE FUTURE

―⁂―

Matthew 24, Mark 13 & Luke 21

The apostles were suddenly all shook up and greatly concerned about the future of their nation, their religion and especially their own personal futures. They had good reason for their anxiety. Jesus had just blown their minds into a state of confusion and doubt. He had made an outlandish statement which they had found hard to believe. Their temple, He said, was to be totally destroyed. In the modern vernacular they would have probably said, "Lord, you have got to be kidding!"

They were so proud and in awe of the temple complex and all that it stood for and it was only now being completed; a very impressive building of great size and beauty. The Lord must have been mistaken about its coming destruction. It simply must not be destroyed; it was, after all, the house of God and was paramount to His presence and His continued blessing and protection upon them as a chosen people. Their existence as a nation was linked dependently to their religious faith and the kind providence of their God. They had heard other troublesome and hard-to-believe utterances from His lips, but this one shook them the most. Surely God would not allow it to happen.

Jesus Foretold His Future

Jesus had been full of bad news in those last months. In addition to pronouncements of destruction of the city and its temple, He had also insisted that He must go to Jerusalem and be killed. At least that news was tempered with repeated promises that He would return to them and reward them for their discipleship (Mt. 16:27). He was going to have *His day (Luke 17:24)* when He would be *revealed (Luke 17:30)* and would gather His own to Himself (Luke 17:31f). *His day* would be a period of renewal during which He would sit on His glorious throne with the apostles ruling over the tribes of Israel (Mt. 19:28). If the city and the temple were to be destroyed, at least they had that to look forward to.

Thus, later, when four of them, Peter, James, John and Andrew (Mk. 13:3) discussed these things, they were rightfully concerned about the timing of them. They assumed there was a relationship between the destruction of the city and His announced return after death. They eagerly asked, *"When will these things be (the destruction of the temple)? And what will be the sign of Your coming?"* Evidently, they assumed He would not let the city and temple remain in utter destruction very long. He would come back and effect their restoration under His reign. So they asked, "What shall we be looking for in order that we may know when you are about to return?"

Jesus Foretold the End of the Age

Jesus had also periodically talked to them about the end of the ages. When He was adamantly headed for Jerusalem for the last time, the apostles had thought that *"the kingdom of God was going to appear immediately" (Luke 19:11)*. That would be the beginning of a new age. They were wrong in their belief that it would appear immediately so He told them a parable to correct their thinking. Through the parable He taught them that He must first go away *"to a distant country" (Luke 19:12)* to receive His kingdom (Luke 19:15) and then He would return and effect the end of the age. Thus it was also understandable for them to ask, *"What will be the sign of the end of the age?"* Their second and third questions were really one, *"What will be the sign of Your coming and (which would also be a sign) of the end of the age" (Mt. 24:3)?*

Jesus Foretold of Much Deception

The primary and immediate concern Jesus had for His apostles was that even they might be deceived about these predicted future events. This is an element in the Olivet Discourse which has not received the attention it deserves. Before He answered their questions He said to them, *"See to it that no one misleads you, for many will come in My name...and will mislead many" (Mt. 24:4-5)*.

Jesus understood and forewarned that even those closest to Him, the very foundation stones of the Christian church, could be deceived about the fulfillment of prophetic events because there will be many deceivers who will come in Christ's name from within the ranks of the Christian faith and church. Sadly that is an element in Jesus' prophecy that is being fulfilled today. Misinterpretation and deception about what Jesus and the Bible teaches about the future has been and is now in our generation a serious problem of large proportions.

Jesus Foretold Specific Areas of Deception

The specific details that Jesus presented in Matthew 24 and Luke 21 were given because they were matters about which He thought His apostles might be deceived. Let us be forewarned by Jesus to avoid being deceived about these same things.

False Christs

"*For many will come in My name, saying, 'I am Christ,' and will mislead many*" (Mt. 24:5).

We shudder at the memory of David Koresh and Jimmy Jones and too long a list of others throughout the annals of church history. Anyone who announces himself to be the Christ or the reincarnation of Jesus or who purposefully creates an environment and uses manipulative teachings to encourage others to say that he is the Christ, must be avoided quickly and totally.

Supposed Imminence

Pretribulationalists preach imminence harder than any other group. By imminence they mean that Christ could come at any moment and, further, that He is coming very soon. Jesus said, "*See to it that you be not mislead; for many will come in My name, saying,...'the time is at hand;' do not go after them*" (Luke 21:8).

This is one of the biggest deceptions being promoted in our day. Multitudes of well-meaning, faithful, wonderfully dedicated Christians are deceived by proclaimers of imminence. Jesus kept repeating that they will come *in His name*. This deceptive message of imminence is being preached by loving, hard working and faithful pastors and other Christian teachers whose intent is not to deceive—but they unwittingly do so because they themselves have been deceived.

Every pretribulationalist is deceived and promoting deception by divorcing the rapture from the actual coming presence (parousia) of Christ to the earth.

It is a serious matter for the church to announce in every generation a premature rapture of the saints and a partial and secret return of Christ and, then, each generation discovers it has been told a lie when these things do not occur.

God has revealed specific signs and events that are meant to alert the Christian community when His coming will be near. When these specific signs occur, then, and only then, will the Lord's return be imminent. These signs have not yet occurred and there is no valid reason for saying that the Lord's return is near.

One may be a great pastor, a powerful and gifted evangelist, a person gifted in many areas of ministry, but still be a misguided and misleading teacher of prophecy. Remember, Jesus found it necessary to alert even His apostles to the possibility of being deceived; He was concerned that *"even the elect"* might be misled (Mt. 24:24).

Dr. Jack VanImpe, Hal Lindsey, Dave Breese, Jerry Falwell, Arno Froese, Tim LaHaye etc. etc. are all devoted servants of the Lord and brothers in the family of God who are winning souls, teaching the Word and living the life of faith in the Lord Jesus. However, in proclaiming that *"the time is at hand"* for the Lord to surely come in this generation they are deceiving multitudes and the Lord says of such, *"do not go after them."*

Wars and Rumors of Wars

It is baffling to me that so very many Bible teachers, preachers, prophecy writers and the like continue to cite wars and rumors of wars as signs of the end. Aside from the fact that in Matthew 24:4-28 Jesus listed such events that would precede the destruction of Jerusalem, He plainly said of wars, *"That is not yet the end."* Nevertheless, whenever there is a threat of war, especially in the middle east, a host of ministries cannot resist the opportunity to write articles and mail ministry brochures to solicit support for their ministries by raising the question, "Will this war or threat of war be a prelude to Armageddon?"

Famines and Earthquakes

Much of what was said about wars and rumors of wars could be repeated in reference to famines and earthquakes. No matter how frequently they occur they are not signs of the end. They are characteristic activities of this age. They become signs only if and when they are world wide in scope and severity. They are only *"the beginning of birth pangs"* and the event to be born is the destruction of the temple not Jesus' return. Anyone who tries to apply these signs (Mt. 24:4-28) to the end times is a deceiver who does not take Jesus' words literally.

Proclaiming A Pretribulational Rapture

We shall deal more extensively with this deception in a later chapter. We shall then prove that the great tribulation predicted by Jesus in Matthew 24:15-28 pertained only to Israel and it occurred in AD 67-70. Therefore the return of Christ and the rapture must be posttribulational as specifically stated by Jesus in Matthew 24:29.

Matthew 24:39-41 also affirms that the pretribulational rapture is a deceptive teaching. Jesus said that the taking of one of two from the field or the mill (in the rapture) will occur at *"the coming (parousia) of the Son of Man" (Mt. 24:39)*. The parousia is the time when He arrives on earth and remains present; it is not a secret trip in which He never arrives, but returns to heaven.

Proclaiming A Future Seven Year Great Tribulation

Of the great tribulation of Israel, which occurred in AD 67-70, Jesus said that it was the greatest ever and would not be repeated (Mt. 24:21). Therefore to teach and look for a future great tribulation of any length on the basis of Matthew 24:21 is deceitful and unwarranted. We shall also deal with this subject more extensively in a later chapter.

There will certainly be great tribulation in the end times, especially during the days of antichrist; but it will not be separate from, but a continuation of, the great tribulation of the church which began with the stoning of Stephen.

Proclaiming A Secret Rapture

Neither Jesus, His apostles nor any New Testament writer has said that there would be a secret return of Christ to suddenly rapture the church out of the world seven years before His actual return to earth.

All the Greek words used in the New Testament to designate His coming, by their innate meaning, emphasize the visibility and subsequent continuing presence of His coming.

Anyone teaching and proclaiming a secret invisible coming and rapture prior to and in addition to His actual return to earth is part of that deception Jesus warned His apostles against. *"For just as the lightning comes from the east, and flashes even to the west, so shall the coming of the Son of Man be." "And they shall see the Son of Man coming" (Mt. 24:27, 30).*

The Fig Tree Deception

Untold number of Bible teachers and prophecy *experts* have taken this simple parable and tried to turn it into a prophecy and have given it a meaning Jesus never gave to it and did not intend to imply by it. These manipulators of the Word have rejected Jesus' own application of His illustration and gave it a meaning that is foreign to the text, but supports their carefully crafted eschatologies.

The simple point of the illustration was that when the fig tree and all the trees (Luke 21:29) put forth their leaves everybody is capable of reading that as a sign of summer approaching. Jesus then made the application of the illustration for us, *"Even so you too, when you see all these things... ,"* that is, those listed in Matthew 24:4-28 then the apostles would know that the destruction of the temple is near.

Much of the present hype about the supposed imminence of Christ's coming is due to an unwarranted belief that this parable is about Israel becoming a nation in 1948. That is deceptive teaching which is contrary to Jesus' own application of His illustration.

In these days when many voices are claiming to know the mind and will of God we need to take heed to Jesus' warning, *"take heed that you be not misled; for many will come in My name, saying,...'the time is at hand;' do not go after them" (Luke 21:8).*

The events which embody the greatest deception and error as taught by leading prophecy "experts" are the great tribulation and the rapture. In the next three chapters we shall expose some of those errors in the light of what the Bible clearly teaches.

CHAPTER THREE

THE GREAT TRIBULATION OF ISRAEL

—⚏—

In the previous decade I wrote two extensive letters to Dr. Tim LaHaye raising questions about his teachings in two books that he had written. It has been my practice to attempt dialogue with those holding an alternate viewpoint, in an effort to strive for greater unity in what the church teaches and whereby, hopefully, we may learn from each other. His response was brief and curt. "I refuse to argue about the timing of the Lord's coming with those whose minds are already made up. For we are all going at the same time— <u>you kicking and scratching</u>—me with joy! I'm 'occupying' until He comes by looking for Him. <u>You must look forward to the Blessed Hope of going through the tribulation</u>—not exactly what I could call a pleasant outlook." (I added the underlining).

I have found this to be typical of the pretribulational mind set. They are unwilling to enter into brotherly dialogue on these matters and when they have no valid answers to valid questions they resort to snide remarks and cliches.

As stated in the first chapter most evangelical Christians are confused and deceived by today's popular prophecy teachers and preachers into believing theories about the rapture and the great tribulation that cannot be supported by clear statements from the Word of God.

In order to understand the great tribulation as predicted by Jesus in the Olivet Discourse we need to be knowledgeable of the background of those chapters, Matthew 24, Mark 13 and Luke 21, in which the prediction is recorded.

In Luke's parallel account of Matthew's record of the Olivet discourse Jesus referred to the coming great tribulation of Israel as *"days of vengeance"* and said that it would occur *"in order that all things which are written may be fulfilled (Lk. 21:22)."* All is not used in the absolute sense as our preterist brothers would have us believe. Not every prophecy of the Old Testament was fulfilled by the great tribulation of Israel, but all prophecies that pertained to that event. Jesus' statement presumes that there were Old Testament prophecies that pertained to it.

Thus, a brief survey of Israel's history, including any such prophecies, is necessary to understand the great tribulation.

Threats Of Tribulation

When God took the families of Abraham, Isaac and Jacob and made of them a nation called Israel, He entered into a covenant with that nation promising to be their God and to provide for them a homeland in which they could prosper and endure. There were, however, conditions to the covenant; they were expected to walk in obedient faith before God and be a holy nation of priests to represent Him to the other nations.

Severe consequences were spelled out in great detail if and when they broke the covenant; which they regularly did through disobedience and the worshipping of other gods. Leviticus chapter 26 lists many of the punishments to be inflicted on Israel when she broke the covenant. The most severe consequence was the threat of invading armies that would destroy her cities and her sanctuaries and scatter her people among the nations of the world (Lev. 26:14-16; 31-33 & 38). That threat is repeated in Deuteronomy chapters four and twenty-eight. Deuteronomy 4:30 acknowledges that Israel will be in distress in the latter days. The Old Testament word distress is the equivalent to the New Testament word tribulation.

Daniel 9:26-27

The clearly stated penalties for covenant breaking were no idle threats. Israel suffered the Assyrian and the Babylonian invasions and captivities in fulfillment of these announced consequences.

Daniel was living during the latter captivity but was getting excited for he had read, studied and prayed over Jeremiah's prediction that there was to be a 70 year time limit to the Babylonian captivity and that limit was drawing near (Jer. 25:1-11 & 29:4-10). While Daniel prayed for the fulfillment of Jeremiah's prophecy, Gabriel was sent to him to clarify matters lest Daniel should read too much into the prophecy and assume a more grand and lasting restoration than would be the case (Dan. 9:22-23).

Evidently, Daniel had not read far enough into Jeremiah's prophecy. For while he had forecast the end of this captivity, and that the return of Israel to Judea would include the rebuilding of Jerusalem and the temple (Jer. 30:3), Jeremiah further prophesied of a time, which he called *"Jacob's distress"* (tribulation), which would be a day like none other (Jer. 30:4).

The *"insight with understanding (Dan. 9:22)"* which Gabriel imparted to Daniel was that the restoration following this Babylonian captivity was not to be the final and permanent restoration of Israel as Daniel might have hoped and expected. The rebuilt city and temple (Dan. 9:25) would once again be destroyed (Dan. 9:26) after Messiah comes and is crucified, that is, after the 70 weeks (490 years).

The 70 Weeks (490 Years)

Gabriel revealed to Daniel that after this captivity ends, it would be another period seven times as long (490 years) until Israel's sins would be atoned for (Dan. 9:24). That would be accomplished by the coming of the Messiah after 69 weeks (483 years) who would be crucified (cut off) in the middle of the 70th week.

The countdown for the 490 years would start when a decree would be given that would allow the Jews to return and rebuild the city. Three kings were involved in issuing that decree—Cyrus, Darius, and Artaxerxes. Since it was viewed as a singular decree (Ezek. 6:14) and was not completed until issued by Artaxerxes, the countdown would begin when he finalized it. He reigned from 459-444 B.C.

After 7 weeks (49 yrs.) the city was to be built again as told in the books of Ezra and Nehemiah.

After another 62 weeks (434 years.) for a total of 69 weeks or 483 years Messiah would come to accomplish the promises of Daniel 9:24. Appropriately and right on schedule the 483 years brings one to the baptism of Jesus when, at the age of 30, He presented Himself to Israel as their Messiah.

During the 70th. week of seven years the Messiah made a firm (new) covenant with Israel. The first 3 and 1/2 years He dealt with them in the flesh. In the middle of the week He was cut-off to affect the new covenant; and the last 3 and 1/2 years He offered the new covenant to Israel as He ministered to them through His apostles. As Mark records it, *"And they went out and preached everywhere, while the Lord worked with them, and confirmed the Word by the signs that followed."*

After the Crucifixion and the 70 Weeks

The climax of Gabriel's clarifying prophecy was that, after a period of warfare, a prince would come whose people would destroy the city and the sanctuary once again—leaving both desolate as the people are taken captive or driven into the nations of the world.

Two different persons are mentioned in verse 27. The first one, the *"he"* who makes a firm covenant refers back to the main subject of these verses, the Messiah; and *"on the wing of abominations will come one (another) who makes desolate."*

All of Daniel 9:24-27 has come to pass as was predicted. The 70 weeks (490 yrs.) are past as well as the prophesied destruction of Jerusalem which occurred after those 490 years in AD 70.

No where does the text mention or suggest any gap, antichrist or seven year tribulation. This prophecy has been totally fulfilled and has no bearing on our future.

Jesus Knew and was Guided by This Prophecy in Daniel 9:24-27

It is obvious that Jesus searched the Old Testament Scriptures and was guided by them as He sought to fulfill His role as the Messiah. The Old Testament contained His job description (Lk. 24:25,27). From the time table given in Daniel 9:26-27 He knew when it was time to be baptized and to present Himself to Israel as their Messiah. He knew also when it was time for Him to be *"cut off."* Further, by this prophecy He knew of the coming destruction of Jerusalem and quoted directly from it in Matthew 24:15 to announce that destruction.

There should be no doubt that Daniel 9:24-27 was heavily upon His mind during the final weeks of His life. He sensed that this prophecy was soon to be fulfilled. When He was on

His way to Jerusalem He announced the coming destruction of the city as Daniel had predicted (Lk. 13:34-35).

When He arrived on Palm Sunday He wept over the city and with broken heart said, *"The days will come upon you when your enemies will throw up a bank before you, and surround you and hem you in on every side, and will level you to the ground and your children within you, and they will not leave one stone upon another, because you did not recognize the time of your visitation (by your Messiah)" (Lk. 19:41-44)*.

Later that week He again bemoaned this coming desolation in conversation with the Scribes and Pharisees, *"...Behold, your house is left to you desolate! For I say to you, from now on you shall not see Me until you say, 'Blessed is He who comes in the name of the Lord'" (Mt. 23:37-39)*.

This is the immediate background for what Jesus then taught about the soon coming destruction of Jerusalem and the great tribulation Israel was to experience as stated in Matthew 24:15-28 and Luke 21. There is a sense of urgency about it, a sense of immediacy. Jesus was weeping over and announcing something that was to happen very soon.

Jesus Foretells the Great Tribulation of Israel
Matthew 24:1-28

Chapter 24 of Matthew is one of the most abused and misused chapters in the Bible. Many seem to be blinded to what is obvious in this chapter as they succumb to the ever present danger of forcing a predetermined viewpoint upon the text rather than letting it tell its intended story.

Of primary importance for a correct interpretation of this chapter, one must understand that the main question that was asked by the disciples and answered by Jesus in verses 4-28 was "When will these things be?" The issue being the destruction of the temple. Verses 4-28 are all about the AD 70 destruction of Jerusalem and its temple and the great tribulation of Israel at that time. The gospel of Mark and Luke do not even mention the secondary questions, *"And what will be the sign of Your coming (parousia), and of the end of the age."* It is utterly shameful and irresponsible exegesis when many writers, preachers and teachers almost, if not totally, ignore this primary question and interpret this chapter as though it were never asked and the entire chapter is supposedly about the second question regarding Jesus' return.

Two factors that are very obvious, and unfortunately ignored by most interpreters, confirm the fact that verses 4-28 contain Jesus' answer to the first question.

#1. This is a <u>private conversation</u> with four of His disciples, Peter, James, John and Andrew (Mark 13:3). Jesus persistently addressed them with the personal pronoun *"you"*, thereby, affirming that they would witness and be involved in these happenings; this destruction of the temple and the great tribulation would occur in their life time. His concern was for them. He began by alerting them, *"See to it that no one misleads <u>you</u> (vs. 4)"* and *"see that <u>you</u> are not frightened (vs. 6)."* This use of the personal pronoun occurs in verses 2, 4, 6, 9, 15, 20, 23, 25 and 26 to link all of the events to the apostles lifetime.

#2. Throughout this section Jesus makes <u>periodic time statements</u> that also tie all the forecast events to the lifetime of the apostles and the destruction of the temple.

Verses 4-8

All the events listed in verses 4-8 are commonly taught as being signs of the end of the age and our Lord's return — false Christ's, wars and rumors of wars, famine and earthquakes. Jesus said that these things are *"not yet the end"* (of the temple, let alone the end of the age); they represent only *"the beginning of birth pangs"* and the event to be born will be the destruction of the temple. It is abundantly clear that

Jesus said that His disciples would witness all these events (vs. 6).

Verses 9-14
Jesus then outlined another list of events that were soon to occur—the tribulation and martyrdom of His disciples, a falling away of many, false prophets, lawlessness, love growing cold and the preaching of the gospel in the whole world. Jesus made it very clear again when these things would happen. Verse 9 again places these events during the lifetime of the apostles. The word *"then"* confirms that they would occur during the same time period as the events noted in verses 4-8. And He said that all the events named in verses 10-14 would occur *"at that time,"* that is during the time when the apostles would be tribulated and martyred (vs.9).

Many mistakenly cite verse 14 as a prerequisite to the Lord's return and quickly point to the necessity of preaching the gospel to the whole world as proof that these verses 4-14 and following are about His return. They do not believe that the gospel had been proclaimed in all the world by the time the temple was destroyed. However, the Scriptures affirm otherwise. The apostles were given the responsibility to take the gospel into *"all the nations (Mt. 28:19)"* and subsequently filled with the Holy Spirit in order to witness *"to the remotest part of the earth (Ac. 1:8)."* Four separate texts announce that their mission was fulfilled in the lifetime of the apostles before the destruction of the temple in AD 70—Colossians 1:5-6, Colossians 1:23, Romans 1:8 and 10:18.

"Then the End (of the Temple) Will Come" Vss. 14-20

When all the events listed in verses 5-14 come to pass *"then the end will come"*—the end of what? It cannot be the end of the age, though that quickly comes to mind because of the secondary question (Mt. 24:3) asked by the disciples. It cannot be referring to that end because all the events listed were to occur in the lifetime of the apostles. Besides that, a different Greek word for the end is used in verse 3 from what is used in verses 6, 13 and 14. In verse 3 the word is *sunteleia* which indicates the entire <u>completion</u> of something—the end or completion of the age. In verses 6, 13 and 14 the word is *telos* which indicates the <u>termination</u> or limit of something—the end or termination of the temple.

This is confirmed by what Jesus said next, *"Therefore when you (apostles) see the abomination of desolation which was spoken of through Daniel the prophet standing in the holy place...etc."* Jesus identified whatever was to happen as a fulfillment of Daniel's prophecy which stated, *"Then after...Messiah...is cut off...the people of the prince who is to come will destroy the city and the sanctuary. And <u>its end</u> will come with a flood, even to <u>the end</u> there will be war..."* (Dan. 9:26).

"Then...A Great Tribulation Vss. 15-28

Matthew 24:21 is the first and only reference to the great tribulation of Israel in the New Testament. Men have misunderstood and twisted the nature and timing of this great tribulation in order to fit it into their carefully crafted eschatologies. It is so important to accept Jesus' prediction and explanation of it.

It's Timing

Jesus clearly established the timing of the great tribulation of Israel to be when His apostles will have seen the abomination of desolation foretold by Daniel (Mt. 24:15; Dan. 9:26-27) and Jerusalem surrounded by armies (Lk. 21:20) which resulted in the destruction of Jerusalem and the temple in AD 70. The great tribulation, then, is already past; the prophecy of Jesus has been fulfilled. There is nothing in His words to warrant interpreting this prophecy as awaiting a future fulfillment unless one rewrites Jesus' words or, as many do, ignores their obvious meanings. The timing was at the heart of the disciples' question about the future. *"When will these things be..." (Mt. 24:3)*. Jesus answered their question carefully and fully.

Its Nature

In addition to carefully establishing the timing of the temple's destruction and the accompanying great tribulation, Jesus made four significant revelations about the tribulation.

#1. It was a <u>local Jewish tribulation</u>. There is nothing to suggest a general universal tribulation. This is clearly stated in Luke 21:23-24, *"There will be great distress (trib.) upon the land (Judah), and wrath to this people (Israel)... they shall fall by the sword (war) and led captive into all nations."* Jesus concern was for *"those who are in Judea" (Mt. 24:16)*.

#2. It was to be <u>the greatest ever</u> tribulation of Israel. It would be *"such as has not occurred since the beginning of the world until now..." (Mt. 24:21)*. That statement ties it to Jeremiah's prophecy, *"It is the time of Jacob's distress (trib.)."* That prophecy was also fulfilled at that time for Jeremiah predicted a great day of which he said, *"There is none like it."*

#3. The fact that it was the greatest ever tribulation of Israel also affirms that it will have <u>no future fulfillment</u>.

Some pretribulationalists and others have seen that the evidence is so overwhelming that they must admit that Matthew 24:4-28 was fulfilled in the AD 70 destruction of Jerusalem. However they want to retain their unwarranted belief in a future seven year tribulation and they need this text to support that error so they claim a double fulfillment for this prophecy. Two factors disallow that claim.

We do not have Scriptural authority to claim a double fulfillment for any prophecy.

Some cite Old Testament prophecies that seemed to have double fulfillments. Only one comes to my mind, that is Isaiah 11:14 *"a virgin shall conceive etc."* That had an immediate and a future fulfillment. However that was acknowledged and revealed in and by the Scriptures themselves to have a double fulfillment. Dare we decide and assign a second fulfillment to any prophecies not clearly designated by Scripture to have a second fulfillment? I, for one, do not believe so. Frankly, I do not trust myself to decide which ones do and which ones do not have a second fulfillment; nor do I trust anyone else to do so.

In this case the question of whether some prophecies can have a double fulfillment and whether we have the authority to assign a second fulfillment to any prophecy is moot. JESUS HAS TOLD US THAT THERE WILL NOT BE A SECOND FULFILLMENT OF THIS PROPHECY! Jesus said that this would not only be a great tribulation, but THE GREATEST EVER for Israel. It will be and was *"Such as has not occurred since the beginning of the world until now, NOR EVER SHALL (BE AGAIN)!!! (Mt. 24:21).* There could be two great tribulations, but there cannot be two greatest ever tribulations. Thus, there is no future great tribulation predicted in this passage for Israel or the church. You can take Jesus' word on that!

#4. While the greatest ever tribulation that occurred in AD 67-70 will not be repeated, the tribulation of Israel will <u>continue throughout this age</u>. They were at that time driven into all the nations where the majority of the Jews living today are still to be found. Jesus had said, *"Jerusalem will be trampled underfoot by the Gentiles <u>until</u> the time of the Gentiles be fulfilled" (Lk. 21:24)* which will not be until Jesus returns.

Not the Time of Jesus' Return Vss. 23-27

Preterists believe and teach that in the AD 70 destruction of Jerusalem and the past tribulation of Israel Jesus fulfilled His promises to return again.

Pretribulationalists believe and teach that prior to a future tribulation of the world Jesus will partially fulfill His promise to return.

Foreseeing that men would mistakenly believe and promote such ideas Jesus made it very clear that He would not return at the time of Jerusalem's destruction or prior to the tribulation. He said that those who teach that are false Christs and false prophets who mislead even the elect. His stern admonition was, *"do not believe them."*

The point of verses 23 to 27 is stated in the 27th verse— His coming will be universally seen (Mt. 24:27, 30 & Rev. 1:7) and will be preceded by visible signs in the sky and on the earth (Joel 2:30; Mt. 24:29; Rev. 6:12-17). These signs and His coming will take place after the tribulation of those days (Mt. 24:29).

Conclusion

The great tribulation of Israel as prophesied by Daniel 9:26-27 and by Jesus in Matthew 24:4-28 is now past, having occurred in the AD 67-70 destruction of Jerusalem and its temple. The greatest ever aspect of it is in the past, but tribulation continues in milder forms from time to time and place to place while the Jews are scattered among the nations until the times of the Gentiles are fulfilled and the Lord returns (Lk. 21:24). And Jesus said, "That great tribulation will not ever occur again" (Mt. 24:21).

CHAPTER FOUR

THE GREAT TRIBULATION OF THE CHURCH

Jesus most certainly did not desire or promise a rapture for His twelve disciples. In His prayer on their behalf just before His departure and even though *"the world has hated them"* He said to the Father, *"I do not ask Thee to take them out of the world, but to keep them from the evil one" (John 17:14-15).*

God had often proven His ability to keep His own during the most tribulated times. He closed the mouths of the lions rather than rapturing Daniel out of the den; He kept three young Hebrews from burning to a crisp while in the fiery furnace that was meant to do just that; He gave Noah and his family a joy ride while the rains pouring down around them destroyed the earth.

Before the great tribulation of Israel occurred, instead of a rapture for His disciples He foretold them that they would experience tribulation and even martyrdom (Mt. 24:9). He told them that they would see the abomination of desolation that was to come into their temple (Mt. 24:15) and Jerusalem surrounded by armies (Lk. 21:20); and thus some of them would live through the greatest ever tribulation to be inflicted upon Israel (Mt. 24:21).

Yet the question is often asked and hotly debated, "Will the church go through the great tribulation?" Before we can give an answer, a second question must be asked, "Which great tribulation are you inquiring about?"

If the question pertains to the great tribulation prophesied by Jesus in Matthew 24:21-28 the answer is, "The church in its infancy has already gone through that tribulation." That great tribulation was a local Jewish tribulation and is already past, having occurred in AD 67-70 when Jerusalem was destroyed.

If the question pertains to the great tribulation mentioned in Acts 11:19 (8:1) and Revelation 7:14, then the answer is "Of course, for that tribulation pertains particularly to the church."

As we explained in chapter one there are two lines of great tribulation traced in the New Testament. The first one pertained to Israel as examined in the previous chapter and predicted by Jesus in Matthew 24:4-28. The second one, which we are about to examine pertains to the church and is mentioned in Acts 11:19 as it explains Acts 8:1 and in Revelation 7:14.

Forewarnings of Believers' Tribulations

There are a significant number of forewarnings to the disciples of Christ that in following Him they would encounter tribulation.

Jesus, Himself, did not sugar-coat His gospel. He always spoke of the hardships that may fall upon those who follow Him. At the beginning of His ministry He taught that His followers must enter the kingdom through a narrow gate and then walk a narrow (tribulated) road (Mt. 7:14).

In His final briefing before His crucifixion He told His disciples, *"In the world you have tribulation, but take courage, I have overcome the world (John 16:33)."*

Paul, who bore the marks of the Lord Jesus in his body, taught the early church to be prepared to endure tribulation. He gave the church two hard sayings on this subject. In Acts 14:22 he taught that *"Through many tribulations we must enter the kingdom of God"* and in I Thessalonians 3:3 he wrote that *"...we have been destined for this,"* that is, for afflictions (the Greek word is *thlipsis* meaning tribulation). He further suggested in Colossians 1:24 that there is a certain allotment or quota of tribulation which the church is called upon to endure.

It is no surprise then that, as the Word of God reveals and history bears out, the church was born and grew in much tribulation as was the case in the churches in Thessalonica and Judea (I Thess. 1:6 and 2:14).

Commencement of Great Tribulation

The great tribulation of the church is carefully documented in the Scriptures. God has told us precisely when it began. It began with the stoning of Stephen in Jerusalem. *"And on that day a great persecution (diogmos) arose against the church in Jerusalem (Acts 8:1)."* While the word persecution *(diogmos)* is used instead of the word tribulation *(thlipsis)* the two are interchangeable and have the same basic meanings. *Diogmos* means to be chased or hounded for evil purposes. Such was the nature of Paul's relentless attack upon the Christian church.

Later in Acts 11:19 Luke reports the stoning of Stephen and then uses the word *thlipsis* (tribulation). Unfortunately the translators chose to use the same word persecution as used in Acts 8:1 rather than the better word tribulation. We understand, then, that according to the sacred Word of God the great tribulation of the church began with the stoning of Stephen. From that time throughout its history the church has continued to face great tribulation from time to time and from place to place.

The Acts of the Apostles chronicles the continuation of the church's tribulation by Paul (Acts 8:1; 9:2) and then King Herod (Acts 12:1-4) and then by adamant unbelieving Jews (Acts 13:50; 14:19; 21:30-32; 23:12). Then the Roman Emperors took up the cause and kept great pressure on the church of the Lord Jesus Christ.

Thus the apostle, John, reported that he and the church were *"in the tribulation" Rev. 1:9*. That necessitated the Revelation of its future to be given in symbolic or coded words rather than plain prose. In the Revelation the tribulated history of the church is painted in broad strokes from the ascension of Christ (Rev. 5:6) to His return (Rev. 11:15) as the seals of the seven sealed book are broken. The church is depicted as the rider of a white horse going forth in obedience to the great commission (Mt. 28:19) conquering and to conquer the world for Christ. In its conquest the church will encounter a world that is overcome by warfare, famine, pestilence and wild beasts (evil rulers); all of which will result in many deaths. Many of these who go forth conquering and to conquer will be martyred for their efforts (Rev. 6:9). All of this continues until an earthquake (Rev. 6:12) and signs in the heavens (Rev. 6:12-17; Mt. 24:29; Joel 2:30) signal the nearness of Christ's return.

The Present Tribulation

We have been blessed and fortunate in the United States. We have not had to endure great tribulation. That makes it difficult for us to understand that the tribulation of the church continues. But we have been told that today there are more martyrs for their faith than in any previous periods in church history.

Rev. Richard Wurmbrand in <u>Tortured for Christ</u> tells us that many believers who suffered in communist countries felt that the tribulation had arrived.

American missionaries, when they were still permitted in China, had taught their converts that the rapture would remove them before the great tribulation began. When the communists took over in China the Chinese Christians wrote to their American friends, "We are in tribulation; did we miss the rapture?"

In the October 1991 issue <u>The Church Around the World</u> flyer reported "Persecutions Continue in Mexico." More than 300 evangelical Protestants were attacked by towns people, which included the beating of two men who were holding a Sunday service. Also members of five families in Santa Ana were dragged from their homes, BEATEN, and taken to a Catholic church where they were ordered to denounce their faith.

Another headline was "New Law Threatens Pakistani Christians" and still another, "Federal Court Allows School to Discriminate Against Christians."

Headlines in other periodicals read, "Pastors Imprisoned in South Korea for Opposing Government Policy;" "Priests Held Incommunicado in Argentina;" "Nuns Accused of Revolution War Tactics in Guatamala;" and "Soviet Court Sentences Baptist Preacher to 10 years in Labor Camp."

Many are familiar with the testimony of Corrie Ten Boom who said, "I went through tribulation when I was in a concentration camp during the last world war." "We must be careful to remember that <u>now</u> at this present time, more than 60% of the world wide Body of Christ is suffering persecution and tribulation."

Corrie also testified, "Jesus does not say 'Don't be afraid, you will be translated (raptured).' Rather Paul in II Timothy 3:12 wrote 'Persecution is inevitable, for those who are determined to live really Christian lives.' I believe that a Christian needs to get ready for hard times."

There may be several contributing factors to the reason we do not experience, as yet, great tribulation in the United

States. First, it may be because of the healthier climate created by the presence and strength of so many churches and believers. The church has been reasonably successful in being the salt of the earth and the light of the world.

Second, it may be the affluence of the world around us and of the Christian community itself. Most of us are not living in poverty and strange as it may seem, affluence seems to help minimize the climate for tribulation.

Third, most of all, I wonder if the absence of great tribulation may be due to our lack of genuine holiness. Are we living the New Testament definition and example of a sanctified and godly life? Are we really that much different from the world in our lifestyle and attitudes so that they would have reason to hate and persecute us? Have we compromised enough with the world so as to not arouse its anger against the church?

I do believe that even in the United States tribulation will probably grow in its intensity and scope in the latter days, especially when the beast of the Revelation appears and the apostasy is in full bloom.

The Conclusion Of Great Tribulation

The tribulation of Israel and the tribulation of the church will end at the same climactic event—the return of the Lord Jesus Christ.

Paul wrote to the church in Thessalonica that God would give relief *"To you who are afflicted (thlipsis—tribulated) and to us as well when the Lord Jesus shall be revealed from heaven with His mighty angels in flaming fire."* Pretribulationalists should take note that it occurs at the revelation, the public visible return of Jesus—not at a supposed seven year earlier rapture.

Thus, the great tribulation of the church (Rev. 6:1-17) ends and the day of wrath begins (6:16-19:21) when the sixth seal events signal the soon coming of Christ.

In anticipation of His coming John is given a vision of the universal church standing before the throne and before the Lamb clothed in their white robes of righteousness with palm branches expressing their peace and victory (Rev. 7:9). This is the church, the final total multitude, which no one could count, from every nation and all tribes and peoples and tongues (Rev. 7:9) who *"have washed their robes and made them white in the blood of the Lamb"* and have come out of the great tribulation which spans the whole present church age. These are the final or full fruits (Rev. 7:9-17) which started with the first fruits, the infant Jewish church (Rev. 7:1-8; 14:1-4; James 1:18).

It seems conclusive that there are two lines of tribulation presented in the Bible, the tribulation of Israel (Mt. 24:4-28) and the tribulation of the church (Acts 11:19; 8:1 & Rev. 7:14). Both are separate and distinct from the day of wrath recorded in the Revelation chapters 8-19.

The great tribulation of Israel began with the destruction of Jerusalem in AD 67-70 fulfilling the prophecies of Dan. 9:26-27, Jer. 30:7 & Mt. 24:15-28.

The great tribulation of the church began in the city of Jerusalem with the stoning of Stephen as affirmed in Acts 11:19 and 8:1.

Both will conclude upon the return of the Lord Jesus. That return, which in the New Testament is labeled His revelation (apokalypse), His appeareance (epiphaneia) and His coming (parousia), will be the time of the rapture which we shall explore in the next chapter.

CHAPTER FIVE

THE REVELATION OF CHRIST & THE RAPTURE

Big Hoss Waters, a Christian brother, presently ministering to his fellow prisoners in a Texas penitentiary, wrote and told me about the first time he had heard about the rapture.

"The first time I heard of the 'Rapture' was when I attended Vacation Bible School at the Church of God. The youth minister had all the kids on one side of the church. The smallest in front and the tallest in back. He broke into tears and said, 'Jesus is gonna come back soon and it may be tonight and when He raptures His church...little kids are gonna wake up in the morning crying, 'Where is my momma? Where did daddy go?' Because they haven't been saved or baptized they'll never see their mom and dad again!" Talk about some squalling kids; two little girls wet their pants, a little boy soiled his. I just wanted to go puke! I was about 15."

It is most unfortunate that Mr. Waters was introduced to a wonderful doctrine of the Bible in this awful way. This was a case of a well-meaning young man using divine truth in a wrong way and not having a proper understanding of the subject himself.

When Paul wrote to the Thessalonian church about the rapture he did not want them to be uninformed or ill-informed about it so that they would *"comfort one another"* by it *(I Thess. 4:17).*

Christians today are not so much uninformed about the rapture, but deceptively misinformed so that they cling to the false hope of being removed from the earth and spending seven years in heaven while a supposed seven year tribulation devastates the earth.

Three Major Errors Taught About The Rapture

There are three major errors generally taught about the rapture.

FIRST, that it will be <u>instantaneous</u>. Zap! And in a split second, without forewarning or voluntary participation, every Christian will suddenly be gone.

SECOND, that it is <u>secretive</u>. The world will not know or see that Jesus has come and will be bewildered by the sudden disappearance and supposed seven year absence of them all.

THIRD, that the <u>second coming is split</u> into two separate trips. They separate the rapture from the revelation, believing that it will occur seven years earlier.

I repeat, and will continue to repeat as long as I have breath or pen or until proven wrong, <u>none</u> of those three beliefs are true. <u>Not one</u> Scripture verse can be found that clearly affirms any one of the three theories stated above.

The Timing Of The Rapture

If we are the terminal generation, as many are popularly saying today, and Christ is going to come in our lifetime, then we ought to be properly instructed and have a reasonably clear understanding of what to expect.

As a starting point we need to understand that the Bible affirms that the rapture will occur at the time of Christ's revelation (apocalypse). These two events, the revelation of Christ and the rapture of believers are closely linked together in the Bible.

The Revelation

The Greek word *apokalupsis* is one of several words used in the Bible to refer to Jesus' return. It means to unveil or uncover something so that it becomes publicly visible. A city may authorize the sculpting of a statue that will be covered and unseen until in a public ceremony the covering will be removed for all to see the sculpture.

The word clearly identifies the return of Jesus as a visible public event.

The Rapture

It is true that this is not a Biblical word, but it is so generally used and well known that it identifies the event we are studying. It refers to the occasion when Christians will be *"caught up" (I Thess. 4:17)* and *"taken" (Mt. 24:40-41; Lk. 17:34-36)* to meet the Lord in the air and then accompany Him as He descends to the earth.

The Order: Revelation Then Rapture

Contrary to what is popularly and erroneously taught by Doctors LaHaye, Lindsey, Van Impe etc. the Bible clearly teaches that the rapture will occur at the time of the revelation of Jesus not seven years prior to it. As I understand it, this has been the historic belief and teaching of the church from its beginning.

The word *apokalupsis* (revelation) is used interchangeably with *epiphaneia* (appearance) and *parousia* (arrival & presence) which, by definition, indicate a visible public appearance and a continuing presence.

Pretribulationalism brought great confusion and division into the church when it was introduced and became popular in the early eighteen hundreds. Without Biblical warrant they split the Second Coming into two trips and separated the rapture from the revelation and said it would happen seven years earlier.

Nowhere in the Bible can anyone find a single verse that says that Jesus will make two trips with the first being a secret coming and a return to heaven to await the second.

Confirmation

Three Spirit inspired persons confirm that the rapture will occur at the revelation of Jesus—not seven years earlier.

Peter, in his two epistles to the church never mentioned the rapture per se. However, while he wrote that the church would experience various trials he assured them that they would receive their *"praise and glory and honor at the revelation of Jesus Christ" (I Pet. 1:7)*. He completely ruled out an earlier rapture when he told them to *"fix your hope completely on the grace to be brought to you at the revelation of Jesus Christ" (I Pet. 1:13)*. If this grace, which is their complete hope, is to be brought to them when He is revealed, the implication is that Christians will be on the earth until the revelation and not removed seven years earlier.

If, of course, they were to die before the revelation then they would receive grace in the form of a resurrection instead of a rapture.

Paul never gave any indication that the church was anticipating the rapture as opposed to or before the revelation. In I Corinthians 1:7 he commended them for *"awaiting eagerly the revelation of our Lord Jesus."* He informed the Thessalonian Christians that they would be relieved of their persecution and tribulation *"when the Lord Jesus shall be revealed from heaven"* not at a prior secret rapture (II Thess. 1:7-8).

Jesus provided the most important confirmation of all. Clearly in Luke 17:30-36 He placed the rapture at the revelation not seven years earlier. *"It will be just the same on the day that the Son of Man is revealed."* He then gives instructions to those who are to be raptured or taken *"on that day."*

Further, in Matthew 24:29-31 He places the gathering of the elect for the rapture after the sighting of Him coming on the clouds.

Nowhere do any of the New Testament writers or early church leaders ever ask Christians to watch for and anticipate the rapture. Nor is there any record in the New Testament of any Christians who were said to be watching for it. They were all watching for the revelation (apokalypse) of Lord Jesus, that is, His appearance (epiphaneia) and coming presence (parousia).

Let us now proceed to follow a step-by-step account of what the Bible says will happen to Christians when Jesus returns and the rapture occurs.

1. The Sighting of Jesus

The return of Christ will surprise the world as it comes upon them as a thief in the night; without foreknowledge and, of course, totally unprepared for it (I Thess. 5:2; II Pet. 3:10; Rev. 16:15). It will come upon them *"suddenly like a trap" (Lk. 21:54),* but when the thief has come and the trap is sprung they will all see Him coming through the clouds.

Christians will have been alerted by the numerous obvious signs that will precede the event and will, therefore, be watching and ready for His arrival.

Many texts affirm the universal visibility of Jesus' actual descent through the clouds to the earth. Jesus foretold it (Mt. 24:30); angels foretold it (Acts 1:11); John foretold it (Rev. 1:7).

2. The Transformation of Christians

After all Christians, living and dead, along with the rest of the world see Jesus coming, even before they are raptured, they will be transformed. It will happen *"in the twinkling of an eye" (I Cor. 15:51-52)*. It is so very important to see that this *"twinkling of an eye"* statement pertains to the change that must precede the rapture and not the rapture itself and certainly not to the return of Christ. Unfortunately even the most popular prophecy teachers fail to perceive this obvious fact or choose to ignore and discount it.

The Change Follows the Sighting
The transformation will not occur until we see Jesus.

This important point is relatively new to me. I have not heard or read of anyone else who has perceived and is teaching it. And I do not know why I nor anyone else have not been aware of this truth before. It is like a diamond lying there on the surface of the Word to be mined. We all missed it while trying so hard to dig deeper or by looking elsewhere.

The confirming text for this truth is I John 3:1-2. This text establishes the order of events to be, first, the sighting of Jesus, then, the transformation of Christians in preparation for the rapture trip to meet Him. John wrote, *"When He appears (is visibly seen) we shall be like Him"* as foretold in I Corinthians 15:51-54 and Philippians 3:21. This will happen *"...because we shall see Him just as He is."* It is the sighting of Jesus that will affect the change which will precede the rapture.

Paul wrote that the transformation is already underway, but it is progressing very slowly because we are beholding His glory as in a blurred mirror (II Cor. 3:18). It will be completed *"at the coming of our Lord Jesus Christ" (II Thess. 5:23)*.

This fact further exposes the error of pretribulationalism. A secret rapture separated from His revelation does not fit the Scriptural scenario. Living Christians must and will see Christ coming to earth before the transformation and subsequent rapture can occur.

It will be a transformation of the whole person which consists of the God-given spirit and the fleshly body it inhabits. The flesh and blood body will become a spiritual body which will be imperishable and immortal (I Cor. 15:50-53) as it conforms to the glorified body of Christ (Phil. 3:20-21). Also the character and personality of every Christian will be sanctified (I Thess. 5:23) so as to be blameless (I Cor. 1:18; Eph. 1:45; I Thess. 3:13; 5:23), holy (Eph. 1:4; I Thess. 3:13) and pure (I John 3:2).

3. The Gathering

After Christians sight their returning Lord and are instantly transformed by Him He will send His angels who will serve as tour guides, supervising and implementing the assembling of the church for their rapture trip to meet Him (Mt. 24:31).

Jesus gave instructions to Christians pertaining to their gathering or assembling for the rapture in Luke 17:30-36. They are to leave immediately without delays, side trips or stops. They are to go empty handed and not pack any bags or try to take anything with them. All their "stuff" will still be there when they return <u>possibly the same day.</u>

Some interpreters deny that this is a statement about the rapture because it would clearly place the rapture at the revelation; therefore, they say that it is the wicked who are taken. Why would Jesus be giving helpful instructions to the wicked with the implication that they have the option of obeying them or not as they are, supposedly, taken away for their destruction?

These instructions are absolutely meaningless unless they are intended for believers and unless there will be time (though limited) and opportunity and the temptation to do the things He warned against.

The rapture will not happen as is commonly and wrongfully taught—Zap! And in the twinkling of an eye every

Christian, supposedly, is gone without his foreknowledge, involvement and cooperation.

I believe that it will be a hasty but orderly departure and that the attending angels and the divine nature and Holy spirit within the children of God will cause them to respond wisely and compassionately. They will not do anything that would harm or possibly kill those being left behind—especially if such are loved ones, perhaps family members.

Some will be on their housetops, in their fields, at the mill or home in bed (Lk. 17:31-36). Jesus did not say anything to or about those who may be driving cars or flying airplanes since they had not yet been invented. I believe that the transformed Christians will have the time, and be expected, to act compassionately and park the car and land the plane as he is motivated by the Holy Spirit and possibly so instructed by the supervising angel. If you as a Christian are the driver of a car or a plane at the time and your passengers are unsaved family members or close friends are you simply going to excuse yourself and send them to their destruction?

4. The Meeting in the Air

"Caught up to meet the Lord in the air" (II Thess. 4:16)..

There are factors revealed that lead us to believe that this meeting will not be very long nor very high above the earth. The general perception seems to be that the rapture meeting with the Lord will take place in the upper atmosphere far above the clouds, perhaps in outer space and certainly out of sight from those left behind. Scriptural revelations about the rapture strongly affirm that the meeting will take place at a not very high altitude and will be visible to those left behind. In support of this consider these factors.

THE REVELATION AND THE RAPTURE

Jesus Sighted Beneath the Clouds

According to Acts 1:10-11, Matthew 24:30 and Revelation 1:7 Jesus will be seen by all the world coming through the clouds. Therefore He will be beneath the cloud level close to the earth when the transformation, resurrection and rapture of the saints occur.

The Air (aer) Beneath the Mountain Tops

According to I Thessalonians 4:16 the destination of the raptured Christians will not be heaven, but the air.

A Greek scholar, Dr. Kenneth Wuest, wrote a book Present Light for Present Darkness which features word studies to help us understand Biblical prophecies. He wrote that there are two Greek words for air used in the Bible. The one is *aither* which designates the upper, rarified atmosphere far above the mountain tops. The second word *aer* is used in I Thessalonians 4:16 which designates the lower, denser atmosphere below the mountain tops. The necessary conclusion seems to be that the meeting will take place beneath the mountain tops and the cloud levels.

How Long Gone?

How long will the meeting last; how long will raptured Christians be gone until they return with Jesus?

My pretribulational brothers, of course, wrongly theorize that after the meeting Jesus will turn around and take all the resurrected and raptured saints with Him all the way back to heaven for seven years. Like a broken record I repeat my oft stated affirmation that there is not a single verse in the Bible that says that the raptured Christians will be taken back to heaven or that they will be gone seven years—not one! The verses most often cited to support that scenario are John 14:1-3. That misunderstood passage is not about the rapture at all, but is a promise to the apostles to return to them after His death and resurrection. He made that very clear in His expanded explanation of that promise in John 14:18-19, 28 and 16:16-22.

The only known agenda for that meeting is twofold. There is to be a marriage of the Lamb to His bride, the church (Eph. 5:27; Col. 1:22; Rev. 19:7-8) and the revelation of the sons (children) of God (Rom. 8:19: Col. 3:4). The church is presently betrothed to Him and living by faith and in anticipation of her marriage when she will be perfected for and by Him (II Cor. 11:2; Hos. 2:19-20). There is no known reason why that marriage should take very long. I do not know that it implies or requires a ceremony of any kind, but earthly ceremonies often take only about twenty minutes. I preached at one worship service where another pastor conducted a wedding after the sermon and before the concluding hymn.

Paul wrote in Romans 8:19 that there would be a *"revealing of the sons of God"* which the created world eagerly awaits. In Colossians 3:4 he informs us that the revelation (Rom. 8:19) will take place when Christ is revealed. *"Then you also will be revealed with Him in glory."* When Christ is revealed to all the world so also will all the children of God be revealed. The world, those left behind, will see the Body of Christ in His presence and coming with Him. It stands to reason that if the world will see the Lord breaking through the clouds and the transformation and rapture of Christians follow that sighting, then, they should also be able to witness the raptured Christians meeting and coming with Him.

This is a conclusion that I did not arrive at hastily or easily; and being a viewpoint that is contrary to what is popularly taught I must amplify this new found truth. The more I read and understand all that the Bible has revealed about the rapture the more convinced I am that the <u>unsaved world, those left behind, will witness the rapture</u>!

Jesus said, *"on that day"* that *"the Son of Man is revealed" (Lk. 17:30-31)* the rapture will occur (Lk. 17:31-

37). And the Bible consistently informs us that every eye will witness Jesus coming through the clouds. And if Jesus will have come into the lower atmosphere below the mountain tops and the cloud level to be seen by the world, will not they also be able to witness the meeting of the raptured saints with Him—thus fulfilling the promise of their revelation as sons of God to the world (Rom. 8:19: Col. 3:4)?

5. The Descent to Earth

All of the above strongly suggests that the raptured Christians will not have gone very far into the earth's atmosphere nor will they be gone for a very long time. There seems to be no reason for a long meeting since Jesus' destination is the planet earth; why should He tarry? In His final statement in the Revelation He said, *"I come quickly."* The word translated come is *erchomai* which means when He is in transit; the trip will be quick.

I know of no Biblical reason why His descent to the earth should not occur on the same day that He is sighted. If so, the raptured saints should also return on the same day that they are transformed and taken to meet Him in the air. It could even be within hours or minutes from the time they are raptured.

Hope for Those Left Behind

The rapture will be a time of judgment and separation, a polarization of people into two categories—the saved and the unsaved, the righteous children of God and the unrighteous children of Satan, those taken and those left behind. There will be some surprises among those taken and those who are left behind.

One of the most difficult questions that we face relates to our obvious concern for unsaved loved ones. How can those who will be transformed and raptured leave unsaved loved ones and go willingly, quickly and happily to meet their Lord? I can only surmise the possibility that the dilemma may somehow be solved in the transformation that will perfect God's children before they depart. Since those left behind will not be left under the threat of any immediate danger, the departing believer may hope that they may be more ready to accept the gospel after all they will have witnessed. It does behoove and challenge us to make the salvation of our loved ones and friends a matter of high priority now. It is also another reason why Christians are instructed not to be unequally yoked together with unbelievers.

Numerous factors offer reason to hope for the welfare and subsequent salvation of many who will be left behind.

Probably all of them will have witnessed the revelation of Jesus as He comes through the clouds. Thus some of the mystery associated with that event will be dissipated and those left behind will have some measure of understanding of what is happening.

Consider that some will also have observed the transformation and departure of their Christian relatives and friends if they happened to be in their presence when it happened. Certainly many unsaved people will be at the sides of some of those Christians who will be in the fields, mills, beds or housetops and other places; and they will witness the instantaneous change in their Christian companions and relatives.

Further, if, as Jesus suggests, there will be time and opportunity to return home from those places, is it not reasonable to assume that there will be time and opportunity (however brief) for limited conversation and interaction with those being left behind? At least two Scriptural passes clearly support this conclusion.

#1. Parable of the Virgins Matthew 25:1-13

This parable is part of Jesus' Olivet Discourse about His return and certainly pertains to the rapture.

The cry goes out, *"Behold, the bridegroom; come out to meet Him (Mt. 25:6)."* Observe that the five faithful and prepared virgins who were to be taken had conversation and interaction with the five who were unprepared and were going to be left behind. Those left behind were not saved; they had no oil (Holy Spirit) in their lamps and, therefore, had not been transformed. Notice also that those left behind tried to go with those who were departing. They begged them, "Give us oil, we want to go with you."

#2. A Coming Harvest Revelation 14:1-16

This passage foretells, I believe, a great harvest of souls that will be reaped after Jesus returns. At least three factors will affect that harvest.

First, there will be the personal presence and witness of Jesus Himself whose main weapon will be the sword (Word) that proceeds from His mouth (Rev. 1:16; 2:12, 16: 19:15) and whose name is called *"The Word of God" (Rev. 19:13).*

Second, there will be the priestly witness of the returning immortal and perfected Christians. Very soon after their departure, probably the very same day, those who departed will be back and possibly reunited with their loved ones whom they had left. Hopefully they will be in a more receptive state of mind to hear the gospel after all they will have witnessed.

Third, there will be the preaching of the gospel by three angels in the sky. Whether one interprets that literally or figuratively the impact is bound to be great.

Conclusion

There are, of course, many unanswered questions regarding the rapture. Will Christians resume and occupy the places they left at work, in the home and in the community? Will they resume the relationships they had before in the family, in social organizations etc?

Let us not get bogged down in questions we can not answer; rather rejoice and be encouraged by the information graciously shared by god in His Word.

The rapture will occur at the one and only revelation (apokalypse), coming (parousia), appearance (epiphaneia) of Jesus. When all the world sees Him coming through the clouds all believers will be immediately transformed and gathered with the resurrected saints and rise to meet Him in the air. When the agenda for the meeting is completed (possibly the same day He is sighted) Jesus and His bride, the perfected church, will descend to the earth.
Jesus presence will provide time, opportunity and reason for many to depart the ranks of the antichrist and to express faith in and allegiance to Christ. There will follow a brief period of conflict during which God will pour out His wrath upon the wicked kingdoms of the world which will reach its climax with the beastly antichrist being defeated in the battle of Armageddon. The Lord with His saints will then rule the present world for a 1000 years at the end of which the final judgment will occur; a new world will be created; and the saints will enjoy eternal life with God living in their midst in a perfect world.

CHAPTER SIX

A COMPREHENSIVE CHRONOLOGICAL OUTLINE OF THE FUTURE

My wife, Evelyn, and I raised five wonderful children. We have fond memories of vacation trips we have taken as a family before they each in turn left home for college. When they were quite young, before we could get very far in what was sometimes to be a long trip, we could always count on one of the restless kids in the back seat whining, "Are we there yet?" We developed a stock answer that seemed to satisfy them for awhile, "We are getting closer."

Like those impatient children and because of the many affirmations that it will happen soon, Christians are asking about the return of Christ and the rapture, "Are we there yet?" "Is it really going to happen soon—in our lifetime?"

All are anxious to know, "When will He come?" In spite of the many voices that glibly affirm, "Oh, yes, He is coming very soon," as though they have had a direct word from the Lord on the matter, the best, the most honest and Scriptural answer that we can give is "We are getting closer!"

Actually, many Christians, under the influence of the false teaching of pre-tribulationalists, are not asking, "When is He coming?" In reality, they are asking, "When are we leaving?" as they look for the rapture rather than the revelation of the Lord. They hold to an unbiblical theory that Christians will be removed from the earth seven years before Christ returns and that it will happen any day now, certainly in this generation.

In order to know where we are on God's calendar we need to know what is on that calendar; what has God pre-announced for us to look forward to? In this chapter we shall present a brief synopsis of all the events that are scheduled to occur in the future; those which we can know with reasonable certainty because they are plainly, and some of them profusely, taught in the Bible. These are the milestones that will help us know where we are at each stage in God's orchestrated plan for the future. We shall present these events under three categories: SIGNS—Those events that will occur before Christ returns; THE MAIN EVENT—The Second Coming of Jesus; and AFTERWARD— The events that will follow the Lord's return.

SIGNS: EVENTS PRIOR TO THE SECOND ADVENT

Before we list the events that will effectively serve as signs that will alert believers when Christ is about to return, it is enlightening to understand what Jesus had to say about signs.

Jesus Talks About Signs: The Fig Tree Parable

In Matthew 24:32-33 Jesus used a simple illustration to scold His generation because they could easily read the natural signs of the changing seasons but could not read the spiritual signs of the times. The implication was that the spiritual signs of the times should be as easily perceived as the natural signs of summer. He used the fig tree as an object lesson. He was not making a prophecy; it was not a statement about Israel's future as some believe and teach. Those who view this simple illustration as a prophecy about Israel becoming a nation are deducing from it, or introducing into it, meanings other than what Jesus intended. Jesus Himself told us the point of the parable when He said, *"Even so you too, when you (apostles) see all these things (vss. 4-28), recognize that he (or it, the temple destruction) is near, right at the door."* Every Greek scholar knows, and many Bible translations note in their margins, that *estin* can be translated *he is* or *it is*. Since Jesus was the speaker—if He were speaking of His return He would not likely say, "He is near," but rather, "I am near" or "the Son of Man is near" as in verse 37. The main question which He was answering was, "When will the temple be destroyed?" We dare not add to Jesus' illustration any meanings other than what He intended and stated.

Jesus simple point was that as easily as men were able to discern the signs that foretell the change of the seasons they should as easily read the spiritual signs that foretell what God is doing.

Signs are not puzzles that have to be solved or mysteries which only a select few can understand if and as they study long and hard or are given special revelations. The signs which God provides to alert His people to coming events will be of such magnitude and visibility so as to be easily seen and understood by the average alert layman as well as the most educated theologian or scholar. Signs are open and observable acts of God that will be out there for all to see.

Spiritual Apostasy: The End Times Climate

The Bible tells of a period of time called the apostasy. This is not a precisely dated event. It describes the spiritual climate of the world in the end times when the Lord will return and the signs preceding His return will occur.

The word *apostasia* denotes a complete, deliberate separation from something. In marriage it is a divorce. In the military it is an AWOL. In this case it is a separation from or denial of the true faith in the living God and His Son Jesus.

Paul forewarned the young pastor Timothy that *"...the Spirit explicitly says that in later times some will fall away from the faith..." (I Tim. 4:1)*. It is one of the two things which Paul said must occur before the Lord returns; the other being the rise of the lawless one (II Thess. 2:1-2).

An Earthquake and Heavenquakes

The first signs that will tell the Christian community that the Lord's return is imminent will be a world wide earthquake and the shaking of the heavens that will visibly be evident in the sun, moon and stars.

Evidently, in the end times the universe will begin to show its age and to lose its cohesiveness and stability which will continue to be evident in the trumpet and bowl events. All will culminate in the final judgment as the present heavens and earth are made new or replaced by the new heavens and earth.

The earthquake will be universal in scope and will seriously effect the earth's topography. It will move every mountain and island out of their places. These events, which will occur during the sixth seal period, are presented as signs that will precede and announce that Christ's return is imminent and are forecast in Joel 2:30-31, Matthew 24:29-31, Acts 2:19-21 and Revelation 6:12-17.

3 and 1/2 Years of Prophetic Ministry
by the Lord's Two Witnesses

During the same sixth seal period in which the quakes shake the earth, two Spirit-filled and divinely empowered prophets will be raised up (Rev. 11:3-14). They will alert and prepare the Christian community to resist the beastly king, commonly called the antichrist; and they will call mankind to repentance in readiness for the coming of the Lord.

Their tenure of 1260 days will probably begin sometime before the beast comes to power. It is he who will then kill or have killed these two witnesses. His gloating over their demise will be short lived. After 3 and 1/2 days the world will be startled and terrified as they witness these men coming to life and ascending to heaven as a voice calls them to that place.

A great earthquake will destroy a tenth of the city of Jerusalem and kill 7,000 people. The survivors will be terrified and give glory to the God of heaven.

Their ascension will be a living parable reminding all Christians that they will shortly be immortalized and similarly ascend to meet their returning Lord in the air.

Neither I nor anyone else knows who those witnesses will be. Since they are not named and there is no statement to say, or even suggest, that they will return from the past, I believe we are to assume that they will be men raised up in the last generation.

The 3 and 1/2 Year Reign of Antichrist

The lawless one in II Thessalonians 2:1-12 is linked closely with the apostasy and will be on the scene when Christ appears. The apostasy will likely create an atmosphere conducive to the rise of the lawless one (generally believed to be the antichrist of I John 2 and the beast of Revelation 13). Many will leave the faith to follow the lawless one and, thereby, hope to avoid being killed.

This beastly antichrist will be identified, not by the number 666, but by three well defined means: by his death and subsequent resurrection (Rev. 11:7; 13:3, 14); by his declaration of divinity (II Thess. 2:4) and by his display of signs and wonders (II Thess. 2:9).

His 3 and 1/2 year reign will end when he is defeated by Christ at Armageddon after His return. The tale of the antichrist-beast-lawless one is told in II Thessalonians 2:1-12, I John 2:18-22 and Revelation 11:7 and 13:1-19:21.

The Fall of Mystery Babylon

In the end times a great city, that is, one that is large, prosperous and powerful, with the code name of Babylon, will lead the nations of the world into physical and spiritual harlotry during the beast's reign.

The majority of scholars and prophecy teachers believe that this city is Rome; others believe, with some good reasons, that it is Jerusalem. Since Babylon is the code name for the city it is certainly not Babylon in Iraq.

A fourth possibility exists that is seldom considered. Since Revelation 17-19 foretells the city's judgment in the end times prior to the Lord's return, it may not necessarily refer to either Rome or Jerusalem, but to an unnamed city, whichever one may then occupy the place and circumstances described in chapters 17-18. In my inability to identify the harlot city with 100 percent certainty I am comforted by the fact that John himself, after viewing the woman, said, *"I wondered greatly."* Even he did not know the identity of the woman.

It is certain that the harlot city will have fallen before the return of Christ because it is the beast and ten allied kings and their armies who will be used of God to affect her fall (Rev. 17:16-17). The tale of this harlot city, which is told in Revelation 14:8 and 17:1-19:6. concludes with an appropriate celebration in heaven of her fall (Rev. 19:1-6).

Six Trumpets: A Cluster of Natural Disasters

The first six trumpeted events will be similar in nature to the sixth seal events. They will be continuing results or expressions of the shaking of the powers of the heavens (Rev. 8:6-9:21).

The first four continue to be *"wonders in the sky" (Joel 2;30)* in the form of a *hail storm* that will destroy a fraction of the earth's vegetation; a *great meteorite* that will fall into the sea and destroy a fraction of the ships and life therein; a *great star* that will fall and disintegrate and poison the fresh waters, killing many people and *unusual darkness* that will strike the earth for a third of the day and night.

The fifth and sixth trumpeted events continue to be *"wonders...on the earth" (Joel 2:30)* that will strike mankind directly and result in many deaths. A plague of *supernatural locusts (Rev. 9:1-11)* with scorpion like tails will inflict men having the mark of the beast with such pain that they will wish to die but cannot. They will be active for five months, but the pain they inflict will prevail after their departure.

Following the locusts, two hundred million riders on horse-like creatures will kill 1/3 of mankind with fire, smoke and brimstone coming from the horses' mouths and tails (Rev. 9:12-21).

THE MAIN EVENT
THE PERSONAL RETURN OF JESUS
Is His Coming Imminent?

Have any of the eleven signs mentioned above occurred as yet? Have we experienced a world wide earth-leveling earthquake or seen the star-shaking and sun-darkening heavenquake as yet? Have we heard from or witnessed the miraculous feats of God's two dynamic prophets? Has the antichrist begun to rule the world and destroyed mystery Babylon? Have we experienced any of the six tragedies to be signaled by the six trumpets? The answer to all of these questions must, obviously, be "No!" How then dare anyone say with authority and certainty that Christ is coming soon— in this generation, in our lifetime?

It is a serious matter to tell folks that Jesus is coming if He has not clearly and obviously confirmed that to be so.

When a teacher, preacher or writer announces a date, even if that date is as broad as a generation, he assumes the role of a prophet. Deuteronomy 18:21-22 affirms that God requires 100% accuracy of His prophets else they are to be considered false prophets not sent by or speaking for God. One is advised not to listen to or show respect for those whose predictions do not come to pass.

I, for one, in my writing and public teaching am flashing the yellow caution light. I cannot yet say with any Biblical warrant that He is coming very soon, that is, in my lifetime or in this generation.

The Church's Credibility at Stake

What happens to the church's credibility before the world, which it is seeking to bring to Christ, when the church keeps lying to the world in each generation by saying, "He is coming in this generation" and then He does not come?

Let us not be so flippant and casual in announcing His coming until we see the signs which are foretold in the New Testament that will precede and announce His coming. They will be large, impressive and obvious for all to see.

I agree with Ed Hindson who wrote in his book, The New World Order, "When you study the facts of prophecy, be sure that you distinguish them from the assumptions you draw and the speculations you make. While we would all like to believe that our Lord will come in our lifetime, it is presumptuous to assume that we are the terminal generation."

To announce His coming before any or all of these events have occurred is discourteous to Christ, deceitful, presumptuous and embarrassing for the church. It will happen on schedule; it is a fixed date known to God. When it becomes imminent it will be obvious to all alert and faithful Christians.

Are we there yet? All that we can answer at the present time is what we have always told our impatient kids as we traveled, "We are getting closer!" *"Amen. Come, Lord Jesus" (Rev. 22:20)!*

The Final Sign

The final sign will be the most convincing of all. It will be the actual sighting of Jesus breaking through the clouds beneath the mountain tops on His way to planet earth.

Jesus had foretold His return in unambiguous terms. He made His first clear statement about it when He began to reveal to His disciple that He would suffer, die and be raised again from the dead. He said that He would return *"in the glory of the Father"* (with honor, prestige and praise); and *"with His angels"* (in display of His authority and power); as the judge of every man (Mt. 16:27).

Just prior to their departure for Jerusalem, where His suffering and death would occur, He spoke of *"The day that the Son of Man is to be revealed."* The verb *apokalupto* defines His return as a visible public appearance. He also clearly indicated that the rapture would occur at the time of Jesus' revelation for He gave instructions for those who would be taken (Luke 17:31-36).

His major statement about His return is found, of course, in the Olivet Discourse recorded in Matthew 24-25, Mark 13 and Luke 21. However, not the whole of these chapters is about His Second Coming. Large segments, such as Matthew 24:4-28, are about the destruction of Jerusalem and the temple which will be the time of the great tribulation of Israel.

In the Olivet Discourse He gave us the sequential order of events that cluster around His return. There will be a *great tribulation* of Israel (Mt. 24:4-29); then *signs* in the sky (Mt. 24:29) and on earth will signal the nearness of Christ's return. Following the actual *sighting* (Mt. 24:30) of Him coming through the clouds He will send His *angels to gather* the elect for their *rapture trip* to meet Him

(Mt. 24:31). Departure from this clearly established order of events has caused good Christian brothers like Hal Lindsey, Dr. Tim LaHaye, Jack VanImpe, John Hagee and a host of others to develop a warped and confusing eschatology and in turn have led many astray.

Six New Testament Truths About the Second Coming

There are two key texts which must certainly control and determine what we believe about Jesus' return. An angel in Acts 1:11 affirmed that His return will be a reversal of His ascension. He will return in just the same way and circumstances as He departed. Revelation 1:7 basically affirmed the same details announced at His ascension. Six clear truths about the Second Coming emerge from all the texts related to that subject. #1. His return is *certain*. #2. His return will be *personal*. Jesus Himself, the One who was crucified, buried, resurrected and ascended into heaven is coming back. #3. His destination will be *the earth*. Every promise of His return assumes, and therefore, does not find it necessary to specifically say that He is coming back to the earth. His ascension was from the earth into heaven and His return will be from heaven back to the earth. #4. His return will be *universally visible*. There will be no secretive returns. Almost all the second advent texts emphasize the visibility of it. Revelation 1:7 eliminates the possibility that it will be an invisible spiritualized return. *"Every eye will see Him,"* the physical eye will see a tangible person. #5. His return will be *posttribulational*. That was the belief of the early church into the second and third centuries. #6. His return will be the beginning of *the day of the Lord (II Thess. 2:1-2)* which many erroneously equate with the day of wrath only.

Five Events Cluster Around His Return: The Resurrection of Departed Saints

There will be two resurrections after Jesus returns. the first will occur as He descends to earth and will involve all Christians who will have died prior to that event. The second will be a resurrection of all the wicked dead after the millennial reign of Christ in order to bring them to the final judgment for sentencing to their eternal destinies.

The resurrection always relates to the body. Christians do not die, their bodies do. Upon physical death, Paul asserts that Christians will be *"absent from the body but home with the Lord" (II Cor. 5:8)*. The body will cease to function while the spirit will be immediately transferred into heaven where it is given a spiritual body suitable for life in that realm. Paul defines that body as *"a building from God...a house not made with hands"* and *"their building from heaven"* in contrast to *"the earthly tent (body)"* which is *"our house in which we groan"* here and now (II Cor. 5:1-2).

According to I Thessalonians 4:14, departed Christians, who will have been resting in heaven since their deaths, will return with Jesus in order to receive new, imperishable, immortal, God-given bodies suitable for the life they will have on earth with Christ for a 1000 years (I Cor. 15:37-38, 52). It will also serve them in their eternal existence in the new heaven and earth (Rev. 21:22).

A Question For Pretribulationalists

Why would Jesus bring departed Christians with Him from heaven if He is going to take them right back there. Why would they receive a resurrected earthly body if He is going to take them back to heaven where they already had a body suitable for life there? I repeat my oft issued challenge which no one has yet proven to be wrong—There is no Scriptural text that says that the resurrected and the raptured Christians will be taken to heaven when Jesus returns.

The Transformation of Living Saints

We shall comment only briefly of this transformation and subsequent rapture since we expanded on these subjects in a previous chapter. I John 3:2 reveals that the transformation will take place when and because living Christians will see Jesus returning. Philippians 3:21 and I Corinthians 15:50-54 define the change as making the body imperishable, immortal and spiritual like the Lord's own glorified body.

The Rapture of Living Christians

Whenever Christ returns visibly and the first resurrection takes place the rapture will also occur (I Cor. 15:50-54; I Thess. 4:13-17). As written more extensively in a previous chapter, the rapture will occur during the revelation of Jesus and will not be instantaneous. Christians will have a limited time in which to respond cooperatively with the assisting angels and, evidently, sufficient time to be tempted to return home from wherever they may be at the time (Luke 17:30-36).

The destination of the raptured ones will be the air beneath the cloud cover and the mountain tops (I Thess. 4:17). There they will be married to the Lamb with whom they shall co-exist forever.

The Adoption of the Children of God

Three texts relate to the concept of adoption. No one becomes a son or child of God by adoption. Jesus said that one must be born into the family of God (John 3). Romans 8:23-25 clearly indicates that no one has yet received his adoption; it awaits us in the future. The adoption is akin to the bar mitzvah when a son matures and enters into adulthood and receives his spiritual inheritance. It will include the experience of resurrection or what Paul calls *"the redemption of our body" (Rom. 8:23).*

Galatians 4:1-7 clarifies the fact that one who is already a child of God is an heir, but will not receive his inheritance *"until the date set by the father" (Gal. 4:2)*. To *"receive the adoption as sons"* means to receive the inheritance as sons.

Ephesians 1:5 is better understood by reversing the word order. The sense of the verse is that as sons God predestined us to adoption, that is, *"that we should be holy and blameless before Him" (Eph. 1:4)*.

The Revelation of the Children of God

The resurrection, the rapture, the adoption and the revelation of the sons of God are related events. The adoption and the revelation of the sons of God occur in conjunction with the resurrection and the rapture. The revelation of the sons of God is the public display and confirmation by God to all the world those who truly are His children.

The timing of this event is very clear in Colossians 3:4 *"When Christ, who is our life, is revealed, then you also will be revealed with Him in glory."*

Contrary to what is commonly believed and taught, the rapture and the meeting of believers with their Lord in the air will not be secretive or a mystery to those left behind. They will witness the children of God in the presence of and coming with the Lord.

AFTER THE SECOND ADVENT

As we continue our comprehensive outline of what the Bible reveals about the future, it is amazing and a bit overwhelming to see how much God has revealed about what will occur after Christ's return.

A Great Harvest

As a result of the powerful word of God from Jesus Himself (Rev. 1:16; 19:15) and the priestly ministries of the perfected and returning saints (Rev. 1:6; 5:10), plus the dramatic preaching of three angels in mid heaven, there will be a great harvest of converts to Christ. According to Revelation 14:13 it is anticipated that many of those converts may be killed as a result of their desertion from the antichrist to the true Christ. In a vision John saw those martyred converts standing before God in their blessed and restful state holding harps and singing the songs of Moses and the Lamb (Rev. 14:1-16; 15:2-4).

The Day of Wrath

The day of wrath will be in progress when the Lord returns, having begun with the sixth seal events—the earthquake and the shaking of the heavens (Rev. 6:12-17).

It will have included the six natural calamities (trumpets) that immediately precede Jesus' return at the sounding of the seventh trumpet. These events were designated as the third woe in Revelation 8:13 and 11:14.

Five finishing Bowls of Wrath

After the harvest of souls to Christ there will be a second harvest as God will strike the wicked of the earth whereby He will destroy the beast and his kingdom. A summary forecast of the bowls of wrath is given in Revelation 14:17-20 with the details presented in Revelation 16:1-21.

The fact that Jesus will have come before these bowl events occur and will be present when they occur is confirmed in Revelation 14:10 by one of the preaching angels who forewarns that all beast worshippers, along with the beast, will *"drink of the wine of the wrath of God, which is mixed in full strength in the cup of His anger; and he will be tormented with fire and brimstone (the fiery judgments of God) in the presence of the holy angels and in the presence of the Lamb" (Rev. 14:10).*

There will occur in rapid succession an epidemic of malignant and loathsome *sores* that will afflict only those who worship the beast. That will be followed by the *sea* (Mediterranean or oceans) *turning to blood* and killing all life therein. The same thing then occurs in all the *rivers and springs* which will deprive mankind of clean, fresh water and make purification of all drinking water necessary.

After being deprived of fresh water the *sun* will become *scorching hot* thereby increasing the torment of the previous plagues. Then the blazing hot sun will be darkened and the whole kingdom of the beast afflicted with *unusual darkness* (Rev. 16:1-11).

Armageddon, The Sixth Bowl of Wrath

Having reigned for about 3 and 1/2 years only to be challenged by this intruder from space, and now with His kingdom in disarray and rapidly being decimated, he is frustrated, frantic and dangerous. Inspired by Satan he and the false prophet, by means of unclean spirits, will persuade at least ten kings of the earth (Rev. 17:12) and their armies to gather at Armageddon (16:16) with the purpose of warring against Christ and His army (19:19). It should be obvious that Jesus will have come before this else they would hardly gather for that purpose.

The river Euphrates will be dried up by the Lord to accommodate this assembly. No actual battle is described or even acknowledged. The text hastens to announce the disposition of the losers. The beast and false prophet will be cast alive into the lake of fire. The rest of the kings and their armies will be killed by the word of Christ and their bodies devoured by the birds of the air (Rev. 19:17, 18, 21).

Armageddon has been built up by over-zealous teachers and misinformed persons into something it is not to be. It will not be a third world war that pits blocs of nations against each other. It will not occur before Christ returns as a sign of His coming. It will be a final foolish effort by the beast and his allies to defeat the invading King of kings who will take possession of the kingdoms of the earth.

The Millennial Reign of Christ

Until and unless proven otherwise I continue to believe that Revelation 20:1-7 refers to an earthly reign of Christ. A number of Old Testament texts are thought to depict an earthly millennium—Isaiah 9:6-7; Isaiah 11; Isaiah 65:17-25 and 66:10-33. In addition, Psalm 2 specifically predicts an earthly reign for God's Son. Most importantly, in Luke 1:31-33 Gabriel clearly promised Mary that her Son would be given *"The throne of His father David; and He will reign over the house of Jacob forever; and His kingdom will have no end."* David's throne was an earthly throne; he ruled from an earthly throne over an earthly kingdom.

The keynote of the Revelation is that Jesus will come back to the earth (Rev. 1:7). That will apparently happen during the seventh trumpet period when there will be a celebration in heaven when *"the kingdom of the world has become the kingdom of our Lord and of His Christ" (Rev. 11:15).* Thereafter, in the book of the Revelation He is revealed as being present on the earth in Revelation 14:1, 10; 17:14 and 19:19.

The Final Battle

At the conclusion of the Millennium, Satan will be released from his prison in the abyss and immediately deceive the nations and motivate them to foolishly go to war again against the saints and the beloved city, Jerusalem. Fire will come down from heaven and devour them. This will, in reality, be the start of the final judgment (Rev. 20:7-10).

The Final Judgment: The Seventh Bowl of Wrath

The term final judgment is somewhat of a misnomer. God has already judged all mankind. The verdict has already been announced. *"All have sinned and come short of the glory of God (Rom. 3:23)."* The sentence has also been announced. *"The soul who sins will die" (Ezek. 18:4)* for *"the wages of sin is death" (Rom. 6:23)*. However, praise the Lord, *"He has not dealt with us according to our sins" (Psalm 103:10)*. He has provided a pardon for those who repent and accept this grace made available through the substitutionary and atoning death of Jesus.

At this final judgment everyone will be sentenced to his eternal state according to his previously established state of righteousness or unrighteousness.

Four Stages of Judgment

The final judgment will begin with the judgment of Satan recorded in Revelation 20:7-10 followed by the judgment of those still living on earth at the conclusion of the millennium as recorded in Matthew 25:32-46.

In the process the material universe will be judged as the heavens and the earth flee away from God (Rev. 20:11 & 21:1) as described in II Peter 3:10-13 and in Revelation 16:17-21.

Finally there will be the judgment of the dead who will be raised from Hades and the sea as those places are destroyed. They will be cast into the lake of fire which is the second death.

The Eternal State

After the final judgment (sentencing) everyone will be in a state, place and circumstance in which they will remain for all eternity.

The Unrighteous State

The wicked will be cast into the lake of fire which we commonly call Hell. This is significantly identified as the *second death*. The Bible does not teach that sinners will be tortured eternally in Hell; it overwhelmingly and consistently informs us that they will be destroyed, burned up and consumed or as the Revelation intimates experience the second death. We will elaborate on this subject in a later chapter.

The Righteous State

Those who will have accepted the gracious pardon wrought by Christ will have their names in the book of life and are variously identified as the righteous (Mt. 25:37), overcomers (Rev. chaps. 2-3 & 21:7), the bride of Christ and the new Jerusalem (Rev. 19:7; 21:2, 9 & 22:17).

They will inherit (Rev. 21:7) and inhabit the new heaven and earth (Rev. 21-22) which will feature the personal presence of God (Rev. 21:3) and the Lamb Jesus.

Conclusion

That is the future as I believe the Bible reveals it. After the signs have occurred which must precede the Second Advent, the Lord will be sighted dramatically descending through the clouds at a level and in a way that will be visible for all to see. It will not be a surprise to alert Christians as it will be to the world when they see Him coming.

This one time return of Christ will include the resurrection and the rapture of all Christians who will then be seen returning with Him.

Following His return will be a time of wrath as God pours out six bowls of wrath on the beast and his evil kingdom. At the battle of Armageddon (6th bowl) the beast and his kingdom will be defeated and the Lord will take control of the world for His millennial reign.

After the 1000 years of peace, Satan will be imprisoned and tortured forever in Hell; the universe will be replaced with a new heaven and earth; the wicked will be punished and then destroyed in the eternal fires of Hell and the righteous will enjoy life in the presence of God in the new and perfect heaven and earth.

Having presented a comprehensive outline of what the Bible clearly teaches about the future and having clarified in some detail the events about which there is much erroneous teaching, namely, the great tribulation and the rapture—we shall next attempt to clarify some of the prophetic texts which, as they are erroneously interpreted, have led many popular prophecy teachers into gross error relative to those events.

UNIT TWO

CLARIFYING ESCHATOLOGICAL TEXTS

CHAPTER SEVEN

THE TIME FRAME OF DANIEL'S PROPHECIES

The book of Daniel is heralded as the key to understanding and properly interpreting New Testament eschatology, especially the Revelation. If this prophetic book is mishandled and misinterpreted the whole super structure one builds upon it may be very impressive and, yet, greatly flawed.

This is the case with dispensational pretribulationalism as it is taught by the most popular prophecy teachers and authors. They have built an elaborate and impressive eschatological system based upon a gross misunderstanding of the time period to which some of Daniel's prophecies pertain and by arbitrarily assuming gaps and events that are not explicitly found in the text.

In this study it will be our intent to focus on those factors in the text which will identify with reasonable certainty the time period to which each prophecy pertains and, thereby, discern whether or not it has been already fulfilled or pertains to our future.

It is always helpful to have an understanding of the skeletal structure of any book of the Bible for it, as well as the words, is divinely inspired and helps to convey the intended message.

Daniel 2:5-7:28 pertains to world history written in Aramaic. Aramaic was an international language spoken at that time. This section features Nebuchadnezzar's dream vision of a great statue and Daniel's dream vision of four beasts rising up out of the sea. Both visions cover the same time period as they foretell the rise to predominance of four successive kingdoms that will prevail on earth until they are all finally crushed by a fifth kingdom established by God, the millennial kingdom of the Lord Jesus.

Daniel chapters 8-12 pertain to Jewish history written in Hebrew. These prophecies pertain particularly to the future of the captive Israelites. It is of utmost importance to understand, as the text will show, that chapters 8, 10, 11 and 12 focus on the cruel reign of Antiochus Epiphanes (175-163 BC) and have no relevance to our future.

PART ONE: DANIEL 2:5-7:28
WORLD HISTORY FORETOLD IN ARAMAIC

Daniel Chapter Two: Nebuchadnezzar's Metallic Statue

This dream vision came in answer to Nebuchadnezzar's concern about his future and the future of his kingdom. It outlines the whole of world history from Nebuchadnezzar's day to the millennial reign of Christ.

Daniel interpreted the dream for Nebuchadnezzar. *"He has made known to King Nebuchadnezzar what will take place in the latter days (Dan. 2:28)."* The term *latter days* is a relative term. It does not always refer to the very last days of the age or of the universe. It designates the latter end of any given period of time that is under discussion. It can simply mean *"in the future"* as it is stated in Daniel 2:45. *"The great God has made known to the king what will take place in the future (lit. after this)."*

The time period and purpose of this prophecy is explicitly stated in Daniel 2:29-34. *"As for you, O king, while on your bed your thoughts turned to what would take place in the future (lit. after this); and He...has made known to you what will take place...that you may understand the thoughts of your mind."*

Obviously the time period covered by this vision began with Nebuchadnezzar's Babylonian kingdom. *"You, O king, you are the head of gold (Dan. 2:37-38)."*

"After you there will arise another kingdom (of silver) inferior to you." That was the Medo-Persian kingdom under Cyrus, the Persian, in 538 BC.

"Then another third kingdom of bronze will rule over all the earth." That was the kingdom of Greece under Alexander the Great.

"Then there will be a fourth kingdom as strong as iron." That was the Roman empire (Dan. 2:39-43).

A Fifth Kingdom Yet to Come

The final fulfillment of this vision pertains more to the whole statue than it does to the individual parts and the kingdoms they represent.

"You continued looking until..." These words connote a passage of time. At some point in the future, during the days of a fourth (Roman) kingdom, when it is divided into at least ten kingdoms (toes), a fifth kingdom will strike the statue and destroy all the kingdoms represented by it. The returning Lord will crush and supplant them with His own. His stone kingdom will become a great mountain (kingdom) and fill the whole earth. It will never be destroyed or passed on to people other than the saints (Dan. 2:44).

Daniel Chapter Seven: Four Beasts From The Sea

Forty or more years after Daniel had interpreted Nebuchadnezzar's dream, he had one of his own. His dream covered the same subjects and time periods, but with some significant additional details. The vision came to Daniel when the time was near for the first phase of Nebuchadnezzar's vision to be fulfilled by the Persian conquest of Babylonia.

Four great beasts came up from the great sea. They represented the same four kingdoms represented in the great metallic statue. The focus of both visions was on the latter stages of the Roman empire when it is divided into many smaller domains represented by the feet and ten toes of the great statue and the feet and the ten horns of the fourth beast among which arose a little horn-king (Dan. 7:7, 19-20).Thus the climax of the vision pertained to the Roman empire when it will have ceased to be a unified kingdom, having been carved up into at least ten kingdoms or nations with independent leaders.

The Little Horn-King

An eleventh horn-king will arise among the other ten. He will become greater than they and will overpower the saints (7:8, 11, 20, 21, 25) for a time, times and half a time which is probably 3 and 1/2 years. He will be commonly known as the antichrist (I John), the lawless one (II Thess. 2) and the beast (Rev. 13).

The Revelation informs us that he, along with the other ten national leaders and their armies will be defeated at Armageddon and he will then be cast into the lake of fire (Rev. 19:19-20).Then *"the sovereignty, the dominion, and the greatness of all the kingdoms under the whole heaven will be given to the people of the saints of the Highest One; His kingdom will be an everlasting kingdom and all the kingdoms will serve and obey Him (Dan. 7:22, 27)."*

PART TWO: DANIEL 8-12
JEWISH HISTORY FORETOLD IN HEBREW

Chapter nine must be viewed separately while chapters 8, 10, 11 and 12 form a cohesive unit which devotes itself to a particular time period in the future of Daniel's people, the Jews—the time of Antiochus Epiphanes' reign over Israel in 170-167 BC.

These visions relate to the time when the Grecian kingdom of Alexander was divided into four realms. The initial focus is on the Seleucid (Syrian) and Ptolemaic (Egyptian) kingdoms as they battled each other for supremacy. The visions then narrow to focus on the cruel reign of Antiochus Epiphanes over the Jews; he is introduced as a *"rather small horn"* who persecuted the Jews.

It is of the utmost importance to perceive that the vision recorded in chapter 10 continues into and through chapter 11 and a part of chapter 12 and is an enlargement of the vision given in chapter 8.

And of equal importance is to understand that THE TIME REFERENCES WITHIN THE TEXT CLEARLY AFFIRM THAT THE VISIONS IN CHAPTERS 8, 10, 11 AND 12 PERTAIN ONLY TO THE TIME PRIOR TO AND DURING THE REIGN OF ANTIOCHUS EPIPHANES (175-165 BC).

At no place in the vision recorded in chapters 10, 11 and 12 does the text announce or even imply a change to a different time period or subject as pretribulationalists arbitrarily say that it does at 11:36 or 11:40.

Daniel Chapter Eight: The Ram-Butting Goat

Daniel foresaw a ram (nation) with two horns (the kings of Media and Persia (8:20) conquering other nations in the west, north and south (8:4).

Then he saw a male goat (Greece 8:2). As soon as he became mighty he was *"broken off"* (died) and the kingdom was divided into four parts ruled by four separate kings (Dan. 8:8, 20).

A Rather Small Horn
A *"rather small horn-king (8:9)"* was quickly introduced and the vision then focused on this king who would come out of the Seleucid (Syrian) segment of the divided Grecian empire. Do not confuse or equate this *"rather small horn"* with the *"little horn (antichrist)"* of the vision recorded in chapter seven. That *"little horn"* king will come out of the former Roman empire in the days just before Christ returns. This *"rather small horn"* king will come out of the Syrian segment of the former Grecian empire before Christ's first coming to earth. There is overwhelming general agreement that this *"rather small horn"* was Antiochus Epiphanes IV.

The Beautiful Land (Israel)
Having expanded his kingdom toward the south and the east Antiochus came into and conquered *"the beautiful land"* of Palestine and the *"host of heaven"* who were the inhabitants of Jerusalem (Dan. 8:9-10).

The Indignation
Please note that the whole of Antiochus' evil reign over Jerusalem was termed *"the indignation"* in Daniel 8:19 and 11:36. We follow the action as follows.

Daniel 8:10
One of the sad aspects of his conquest of the Jews was that some of the host (inhabitants of Jerusalem) and their leaders (stars) thought it best to cooperate with Antiochus and they assisted him in his attempt to Hellenize the Jews and to eliminate their faith and religious practices.

Daniel 8:11
He challenged and assumed the authority of the Commander (Prince or religious leader) of the host. Having replaced the high priest, he discontinued the offering up of the regular sacrifices and destroyed the holy place.

Daniel 8:12
He himself took over the priestly function and flinging truth to the ground he did successfully whatever he willed to do.

Daniel 8:13
I believe that the two angels were Gabriel and Michael one of whom asked how long the trampling of the holy place and the host (populace) of Jerusalem will be allowed. The answer was 2300 evenings and mornings, that is 2300 days. The phrase *"evenings and mornings"* is a common Hebrew expression for days. As Dr. Wilbur M. Smith has duly said, "This period of 2300 days is the length of time during which the sanctuary was desecrated by the army of Antiochus Epiphanes, 171 BC to December 25, 165 BC" It covers the total period from the time Antiochus took Jerusalem until John Maccabees took it back and restored the regular sacrifices.

The question concerned the length of time that Antiochus would trample the holy place and the host in Jerusalem not simply the length of time that the regular sacrifices would be stopped.

The Transgression Daniel 8:12
God allowed and used the invasion of Jerusalem because of the transgression of its leaders and citizenry. *"The indignation" (Dan. 8:19; 11:36)* is also known as *"the transgression" (8:12, 13 & 23)*.

Daniel summed up the reason for the indignation of Antiochus Epiphanes' reign over Israel in his prayer recorded in Daniel 9:11-14.

The text confirms what is clearly stated in Daniel 8:19 that the vision pertains to *"what will occur at the final period of the indignation (of Antiochus' reign), for it pertains to the appointed time of the end;"* the end in view being the end of the indignation of his reign not the end of the age or of the world.

Clearly the vision of chapter 8 as well as the enlargement of it in chapters 10-12 has already been fulfilled and has no pertinence to our future.

Daniel Chapter Nine: The Vision of 70 Weeks

We come now to the most critical and controversial vision of the book.

Possibly more than anything else, an arbitrary gross misinterpretation of Daniel 9:24-27 has contributed to the confusion and error that is commonly and profusely taught by many popular prophecy teachers.

This prophecy, wrongly interpreted, is the foundational text on which pretribulationalism has built an elaborate and impressive, but erroneous eschatological theory. They supposedly find in this text things which are not there—a gap between the 69th and 70th weeks, an antichrist who makes a peace treaty with Israel and a seven year tribulation period. NONE OF THESE ARE SPECIFICALLY STATED OR INTENTIONALLY IMPLIED IN THE TEXT.

Circumstances Prompting the Vision

Babylon had only recently been conquered by the Persian King Cyrus.

Daniel reviewed Jeremiah's prophecy that affirmed that the Jews servitude to Babylonia was to last 70 years and that God would release them back to Judea (Jer. 25:11-12;

29:10 & Chron. 36:20-21). He was excitedly aware that the 70 years were completed and Israel's captivity should be nearing the end.

With this knowledge and in great hope Daniel was driven to his knees in repentance and prayer for himself and his national brothers. He repeatedly confessed Israel's transgressions as the reason for their captivity and pleaded with God to keep His covenant and to exercise compassion and forgiveness.

The Vision

Daniel's prayer was interrupted by the appearance of the angel Gabriel who was sent to him as was done once before. Daniel's prayer reflected his expectation and hope that Jerusalem would be rebuilt (Dan. 9:26) as well as the temple (sanctuary 9:17). Gabriel was sent to assure Daniel that those things would happen but to caution Daniel not to expect too much too soon. Gabriel gave Daniel a time table for God's answer to Daniel's prayer and that will establish two important facts.

#1. The atonement for Israel's sins, which is necessary for God to forgive them as Daniel desired (Dan. 9:9, 19), will not occur until seven more units of 70 years or a total of 490 years have passed.

#2. Even though Jerusalem and its temple will be rebuilt they shall not endure. After atonement has been provided and the 490 years are past they will be destroyed once again.

70 Weeks Are Decreed

One must read this prophecy (9:24-27) carefully and guard against reading into the text anything that is not clearly affirmed.

No Gaps or Extensions

It is generally agreed by scholars and prophecy experts that the 70 weeks in this instance are 70 units of 7 years or a total of 490 years. God said and meant 490 years. There is no stated or implied gap in the 490 years; they run consecutively without interruption. The notion that God stopped counting after 483 years and will start counting again at some unknown date in the future is a presumptive invention of men.

Pertains to the First Coming of Christ

There is nothing in this visionary prophecy (Dan. 9:24-27) that pertains to the return of Christ and the end times. A starting point is given for the count down and after 483 years Messiah will arrive and in the middle of the seventieth week He will be crucified and thereby accomplish the atonement promised in Daniel 9:24.

The Starting Point: A Decree

Some quibble over the wording of the several decrees that relate to the return of the Jews to Jerusalem. They distinguish between those that specify the restoration of Jerusalem, those that specify the rebuilding of the temple and those that specify the release of the Jews to return to Jerusalem.

Any reference to any one of these three activities implies, includes and necessitates the intent to accomplish the other two.

In 538 BC Cyrus issued a decree to allow the Jews to return to Jerusalem to rebuild the temple. II Chronicles 36 clearly states that this was in fulfillment of Jeremiah's prophecy; and Ezra 4:16 affirms that it included the rebuilding of the city. The work was interrupted by Artaxerxes until Darius the great reissued the decree and authorized the resumption of the work around 519-518 BC (Ezra 4:24-6:12).

A later Artaxerxes finalized the decree around 459-458 BC permitting Ezra and others to return to Jerusalem with provisions for the resumption of full services in the temple.

It is important to note that according to Ezra 6:14 the decrees of Cyrus, Darius and Artaxerxes are considered as one decree. Therefore the date for the starting point of the 490 years must be 459-458 BC in order to include Artaxerxes' decree.

First Milestone: Restoration of Jerusalem

"From the issuing of a decree to restore and rebuild Jerusalem...it will be built again, with plaza and moat, even in times of distress" (Dan. 9:25). The books of Ezra and Nehemiah chronicle that rebuilding project.

Second Milestone: Messiah Arrives

"From the issuing of a decree to restore and rebuild Jerusalem until Messiah the Prince (comes) there will be seven weeks (1st milestone) and (an additional) sixty-two weeks" making a total of 69 weeks or 483 years. The 69th week or 483 years added to the starting date of 459-458 BC brings one to the date of Jesus' baptism and the beginning of His Messianic ministry to Israel—thus, starting the 70th week of seven years.

The 70th Week

Verse 26 cites two major events that would occur after the 69th week when Messiah appears.

#1. His crucifixion: *"Messiah will be cut off."* According to verse 27 this will happen in the middle of the 70th week.

#2. The destruction of *"the city and the sanctuary."* No specific time is given for this event except that it will be after the 69th week. We now know that it happened about 40 years later in 67-70 AD.

Verse 27 provides some details about the 70th week as follows:

Messiah Makes A Covenant

The main subject of this prophecy and of verses 26 and 27 is the Messiah. It is he who *"will make a firm covenant with the many for one week."* That is the new covenant which Messiah affected and offered to Israel. The one week (the 70th) included the 3 and 1/2 years Jesus ministered in the flesh to Israel and the 3 and 1/2 years of ministry in the Spirit as He worked with and through the apostles as they offered the new covenant to Israel. *"They went out and preached everywhere, while the <u>Lord worked</u> with them (Mk. 16:20)."*

Pretribulationalists teach that it is the antichrist who will make the covenant with Israel. They are in error on two counts. First, the 490 years have long since passed and the antichrist has not yet appeared. Second, after referring to the one who will make a firm covenant the text goes on to say *"and (in addition to that act) on the wing of abominations will come one (another in addition to the one who makes the covenant) who makes desolate."* Pretribbers wrongly identify this second person as the antichrist. Even if that were true, he is not the one who makes the covenant.

Messiah is Crucified Daniel 9:27

In the middle of the week Messiah will be *cut off* and thereby fulfill the promised atonement stated in Daniel 9:24. Many Scriptural texts can be cited which clearly and adequately show that all the promises made in Daniel 9:24 were accomplished by Christ and do not await a future fulfillment. Many confirming passages even use the very words embodied in the promises of Daniel 9:24.

"To finish (restrain) the transgression" was confirmed as fulfilled in Isaiah 53, 54 and 56 and Hebrews 9:15.

"To make an end of sin" was confirmed as fulfilled in Hebrews 9:26, John 1:29 and I John 3:5.

"To make atonement for iniquity." These first three promises are three different expressions of the atoning work of Christ which was accomplished by His crucifixion. As the Holy Spirit announced through Zachariah with regard to the incarnation, *"He (God) has visited us and <u>accomplished redemption</u> for His people...(Luke 1:68)."*

"To bring in everlasting righteousness" was confirmed as fulfilled in Romans 3:21-22 and 5:19.

"To seal up vision and prophet." This is the most difficult of these promises to interpret with absolute certainty. It may be understood in at least two different ways.

#1. To seal means to make authentic and effective. It can convey the idea that Christ has fulfilled the Old Testament prophecies (Acts 3:18; and Luke 24:27-47).

#2. To seal means to close or end something. This promise may simply mean that God will no longer communicate through visionary and predictive prophets. Jesus said, *"All the prophets and the Law prophesied <u>until</u> John (Mt. 11:13)."* This may be implied by Hebrews 1:1-2 as well.

The meaning of this phrase may be found in a combination of these two views.

"To anoint the most holy." I believe that this has been fulfilled in the life and death of Jesus. He is certainly the Most Holy (One) and the Scriptures confirm His anointing. For that see Isaiah 61:1, Luke 4:18-19 and Acts 10:38. The very title *"Christ"* of course, identifies Jesus as the anointed one.

The Destruction of Jerusalem

The only time reference given for this event is that it will happen *"after the sixty-two weeks,"* that is, after Messiah has come. It is an historical event that has been well documented and dated, having occurred in AD 67-70.

In Matthew 24:15 Jesus cited Daniel 9:27 and said that it would be fulfilled (and was) during the apostles' lifetime when they would see the abominations in the holy place and Jerusalem surrounded by armies (Luke 21:24).

A *"prince who is to come"* will destroy the city and the sanctuary. This prince cannot be the same as the one who makes a firm covenant because he is introduced as an additional person other than the covenant maker.

The 490 years that were decreed have long since passed and Daniel 9:24-27 has been totally fulfilled. This prophecy contributes nothing to our understanding of the end times.

Daniel's Vision of Antiochus' Reign Daniel 10:1-12:4

If one does not impose a preconceived belief that this vision (10:1-12:4) pertains to the antichrist and our end times, the text will clearly establish:

#1. That the vision begins at Dan.10:1 and concludes at 12:4.

#2. That the vision covers the same time period (175-163 BC) and subject matter (the reign of Antiochus IV) as the vision recorded in chapter 8. It enlarges on that vision with more details regarding Antiochus' reign in Jerusalem.

#3. There are no sudden changes in the subject matter or sudden leaps into the future end times.

The vision forecasts a *"great conflict"* which was to come upon the rebuilt city. In Daniel 12:1 it is described as a *"time of distress (trib.) such as never occurred since there was a nation until that time."* That is not a reference to the great tribulation predicted by Jesus in Matthew 24:21. The great conflict of Daniel 10:1 and 12:1 was fulfilled by Antiochus' rule over Jerusalem in 175-163 BC while the great tribulation of Israel occurred in AD 67-70 and was called the greatest of all time.

A Time Statement Daniel 10:14

Gabriel announced, *"I have come to give you an understanding of what will happen to your people in the latter days, for the vision pertains to the days yet future."* According to the initial vision (chap. 8) the prophecy pertains not to the end of the world or of the age but to *"the final period of the indignation" (Dan. 8:19)* which is what Antiochus' reign was called. It is this end that is referred to in Daniel 8:19; 11:27, 35, 40 and 45.

Ascendancy of Greece

A shift in power is about to occur. Daniel 10:20-21, which corresponds to Daniel 8:5-7, forecasts the defeat of Persia by Greece under Alexander (11:3). After four more Persian kings (Dan 11:2) a mighty king, Alexander, will arise in Greece. He is the large horn of the male goat in Daniel 8:5, 8 and 21.

After Alexander's death the empire was broken into four segments with the major powers being Syria, ruled by the Seleucids and Egypt ruled by the Ptolemies.

Conflicts Between North and South

The Egyptian kings in the south will battle the Syrian kings of the north for supremacy. Israel will be caught in the middle of these conflicts as these north and south powers pass back and forth. Carl G. Howie writes in <u>The Laymen's Bible Commentary</u>, "Moreover, chapter 11 is a remarkable and accurate narration of Seleucid and Ptolemaic history in the third and second centuries BC." The end result of these conflicts will find Israel under the oppressive rule of Antiochus Epiphanes.

Antiochus Epiphanes IV Rules Israel

Antiochus IV is introduced in Daniel 11:21 as *"a despicable person,"* the same Syrian leader who was presented in Daniel 8:9-14 and 23-26 as a *"rather small horn."*

During his conflicts with Egypt it is noted that *"his heart will be set against the holy covenant, and he will take action and then return to his own land (Dan. 11:28)."* The holy covenant is a reference to the Jews, the people of God. In 168 BC Antiochus marched through Judea and *"became enraged at the holy covenant and took action against them (Dan. 11:30)."* Showing favor to and in cooperation with *"those who forsake the holy covenant (Dan. 11:30)"* he took strong measures to eradicate the Jewish faith and practices in an effort to Hellenize them.

He Desecrates the Temple Daniel 11:31f

Antiochus prevented the normal use of the temple from serving the spiritual needs of the Jews. He slaughtered orthodox Jews in the temple, stopped the regular sacrifices (Dan. 11:31 & 8:3), forbade circumcision, Sabbath observance and the reading of the Scriptures. To top it off he erected an altar to Zeus and offered swine's flesh in flagrant violation of their religious laws.

"An Appointed Time" To End His Rule

As was predicted *"They will fall by the sword and by flame, by captivity and by blunder, for many days (Dan. 11:33 and 8:26)."* This will occur *"until the end time; because it is still to come at the appointed time (Dan. 11:27, 35, 40 and 45)."* All references to the end time or the end of the days in this prophecy relate to the end of the tribulation under Antiochus IV, not to our future.

No Change in Subject or Time

Many, arbitrarily and without textual warrant, assume and teach that Daniel abruptly ceases to be writing about Antiochus and the Jews in 175-163 BC and instead writes about the antichrist and the end times that are yet to come. Some make the break at verse 36 and others at verse 40. No change in the subject matter or the time period is announced or even hinted at. There is nothing in the text that warrants or requires a sudden leap into the last days.

The end of this indignation under Antiochus is forecast in Daniel 11:40-45, *"He will come to his end and no one will help him."*

Michael Assists Israel

It is very important to understand the time period to which chapter 12 pertains. The very first words definitely tie it to the time period covered in chapters 10 and 11. It is plainly affirmed that chapter 12 continues to relate to matters pertaining to the end of Israel's indignation suffered under Antiochus IV. That will have been *"a time of distress such as never occurred since there was a nation until that time."*

For what purpose will Michael step forward and how will he minister to Israel in those days.

#1. To Spare A Remnant

Many of the Jews will die during this cruel period of distress under Antiochus. However, *"at that time"* some, whose names are written in the book (of life), will be rescued or spared. They will live.

#2. To Confirm a Resurrection to Eternal Life

The text does not say or suggest that the resurrection will occur at that time.

All who will die during this period of time will be resurrected when the resurrection occurs. Many will be resurrected *"to everlasting life"* in the first resurrection (Rev. 6:1-6); but others will be resurrected to *"disgrace and everlasting contempt"* at the final judgment (Rev. 20:11-15).

Later Gabriel informed Daniel that his resurrection as one of the *"many who sleep in the dust" (Dan. 12:2)* will occur *"at the end of the age (Dan. 12:13)."*

#3. To Give Insight to Some

Verse 10 again speaks of those who have insight; they will understand these prophecies and benefit from that understanding. They will be *"purged, purified and refined."* They will likely resist and not support Antiochus. They will lead many to righteousness. As it was prophesied in *Daniel 11:32-33 "the people who know their God will display strength and take action. And those who have insight among the people will give understanding to the many."*

#4. To Affect the Maccabean Revolt

Chief among those who had insight and were motivated and helped by Michael was Matthias, an aged priest of the Hasmonian family, who resisted the attempted Hellenization of the Jews and led a growing revolutionary force that defeated several Syrian armies.

His son, Judas Maccabeus, in 165-164 BC recovered Jerusalem, cleansed the temple and resumed the regular temple services. Judas' son, Jonathan, continued what had become a war of independence from 161 to 143 BC.

Final Revelations and Instructions Daniel 12:4-13

In the final section of the book of Daniel (12:4-13) God deals with three matters—the publishing of the book; the question of how long it will be until this final vision is fulfilled and Daniel's personal destiny.

Publishing Instructions

"Conceal these words and seal up the book (Dan. 12:4)."
"These words are concealed and sealed up until the end time (of Antiochus IV)."

After writing these several prophecies in a book, Daniel is told not to publish the book or make the prophesies publicly accessible. This is strange instruction and difficult to understand.

The visions were evidently given for Daniel's personal enlightenment and encouragement. This restriction possibly pertained particularly to the Hebrew section of the book because the fulfillment of these visions was to be in the distant future. The intent was to withhold the book until the time of its fulfillment. Two factors support this. First, Daniel had received similar instruction earlier. In Daniel 8:26 he was told, *"keep the vision secret, for it pertains to many days in the future."* Second, the opposite instruction was given to John when he received the Revelation. *"Do not seal up the words of the prophecy of this book, for the time is near (Rev. 22:10)."*

"Until the End of Time" Daniel 12:4 &

This is a most unfortunate translation; one which has led many to a totally erroneous interpretation of these visions.

In this instance the King James, the NIV and Young's Literal Translation provide the correct translation of this phrase. It is not *"the end of time (vs.4)"* or *"the end time (vs. 9)"* but *"the time of the end"* meaning the time of the end of the indignation under Antiochus Epiphanes. The phrase is thus used throughout this vision in Daniel 8:17-19; 9:26; 11:35, 40, 45 and 12:4, 6, 9.

The Length of These Wonders

The question is asked and answered, *"How long until the end of these wonders?,"* meaning the events revealed in this vision (chaps. 10-12).

Three time statements are given.

#1. "For a time, times and half a time" Daniel 12:7

It is generally, and probably correctly, believed that the phrase means *"for 3 and 1/2 years."* However, it may simply indicate an indefinite but limited period of time.

#2. 1290 days Daniel 12:11

1290 days equals three years and seven months of 30 days each. The outcome or final end of these events will come 1290 days after the regular sacrifice is abolished and the abomination of desolation is set up. These two events occur practically concurrently and mark the climax of the indignation under Antiochus IV.

#3. 1335 days Daniel 12:12

The one who endures the 1290 days of hardship and attains to the 1335 days is blessed because he will have survived the horror and persecution of those days. These are they who will have been found written in the book of life as mentioned in Daniel 12:1.

Daniel's Personal Destiny Daniel 12:13

The final word of the prophecy is about Daniel personally. *"But as for you, go your way to the end (of your life); then you will enter into rest (Rev. 14:13) and rise again (with the many who are asleep Dan. 12:2) for your allotted portion at the end of the age (lit. days)."*

A Summation

The Great Statue Chapter Two

This dream of Nebuchadnezzar is statedly a revelation of *"what will take place in the future (Dan. 2:29 & 45)."* In the days of the fourth (Roman) kingdom God will set up a kingdom that will supercede all others and never be diminished or replaced. It will be an everlasting kingdom. The predicted kingdom is the kingdom of Christ which was given to Him upon His ascension into heaven (Dan. 7:13-14) and of which all believers become a part (Col. 1:13; Rev. 1:6; 5:10 etc.).

The Four Beasts Chapter Seven

The four beasts represent the same four kingdoms as portrayed by the statue.

The primary focus of the vision is on the eleventh horn (king), a little one, who becomes aggressive and abominable.

All of verses 8-12, 18, 20-21, 24-27 await a future fulfillment. They pertain to the time of the antichrist and the eventual coming of Christ who will share His kingdom with the saints.

The Ram and the Goat Chapter Eight

The ram and the goat are clearly identified in Daniel 8:20-22 as Media-Persia and Greece.

The focus and main feature of this prophetic vision is to foretell the cruel career of the rather small horn (Dan. 8:9) who was Antiochus Epiphanes, *"a king...insolent and skilled in intrigue (Dan. 8:23)."* All of chapter eight has been fulfilled in his days. There are no unfulifiled parts in this prophetic vision.

The 70 Weeks Chapter Nine

This prophecy promises that after 490 years the Messiah will have come, been crucified and will have effected the new covenant with Israel.

However, after that the city and sanctuary will once again be destroyed, which it was in AD 70. Whereupon the people were dispersed into the nations of the world.

There is certainly no gap and no reference to a seven year tribulation period in this prophecy. The prophecy in its entirety has been fulfilled.

The Great Conflict Chapters 10-12
Much of this vision pertains to the conflicts between two of the kingdoms which resulted from the break up of the Grecian kingdom, namely, Egypt and Syria. Israel was caught in the middle of those conflicts.

The prophecy then devotes itself to the cruel rule of a despicable person, Antiochus Epiphanes in 175-163 BC.

Many of us agree with Lehman Strauss who wrote, "At least half (I, R.L.K., believe much more than half) of the prophecies foreshadowed in this book, have literally come to pass."

Al Martin wrote of the detailed predictions in Daniel, "Many...were fulfilled in the period between Daniel and the (first) coming of Christ."

All of the prophecies found in chapters 8-12 have been fulfilled (except references to the resurrection).

A forced misinterpretation of Daniel 9:24-27 and wrongly interpreting Daniel 11:45-12:4 as a prophecy pertaining to the end-times rather than to the reign of Antiochus Epiphanes may have contributed more than anything else to the erroneous theories of pretribulationalism.

CHAPTER EIGHT

THE TIME FRAME OF EZEKIEL'S PROPHECIES

Ezekiel was the first man to spot a UFO. However, it was not an unidentified flying object to him. He knew what it was and who it contained.

Ezekiel was a priest and since he was thirty years of age he would have been permitted to become active in the services of the temple (Num. 4:3; 23, 30, 35; I Chron. 23:3) if he were back in Jerusalem. There he would have entered the inner sanctuary of the temple which housed the ark of the covenant (I Kings 6:19; I Chron. 22:19) where he would have met and conversed with God above the mercy seat.

Since Ezekiel was in captivity in Babylon and could not exercise his life long aspiration in Jerusalem, God came in the ark of the covenant to Ezekiel. The strange vehicle in which God visited Exekiel was the ark of the covenant adapted for mobility. God came to Ezekiel atop the mercy seat in a portable ark of the covenant.

God's First Visitation Ezekiel 1:4-3:21

There are three kinds of visions by which God communicated with mankind through His prophets. There were dream visions called visions of the night as experienced by Nebuchadnezzar and Daniel. There were spiritual trances in which the prophet was said to be in the Spirit. These occur within the mind of the prophet who is not physically transported to the places he may visit while in the Spirit. A third kind of vision occurs when one is wide awake with one's faculties and senses functioning normally. A spiritual presence is manifested during the normal course of one's life. It is more accurate to describe this as a visitation rather than a vision. What one sees is an actual phenomenon that is present. This was what Ezekiel experienced.

A storm wind brought a great cloud with fire flashing within and from it. As details became clearer he understood what he was seeing. He understood that God was visiting him in a cloud which bore the ark of the covenant. From above the ark God met and spoke to him.

The conveyance described in chapter 1:4-25 was the ark of covenant with appropriate variations from its original design to express the idea of mobility. This ark was not to be carried, but adapted for flight. A more detailed description of this visitation and of the portable ark may be found in issue 21 of Second Thoughts which is available by writing or phoning the author.

After this initial visitation God visited Ezekiel three more times in this same conveyance as recorded in Ezekiel 3:23; 8:2-4 and 43:2-5.

Ezekiel's Assignment Ezekiel 1:28-3:21

When God asked Ezekiel to stand up so that He might speak to him the Spirit entered into him and brought him to his feet. God then gave Ezekiel his assignment.

Sent to Captive Israel Ezekiel 2:4-3:14

Ezekiel was sent to the captive Israelites as God's spokesman. It was not a very appealing assignment. God forewarned Ezekiel that they had been and would continue to be a rebellious, stubborn and obstinate people—that being the reason for being in exile. Whether they listen or not Ezekiel must deliver the very words of God; they must know that a prophet of God has been among them. The word Ezekiel was to deliver to Israel was not a warm fuzzy message, but one of lamentation, mourning and woe.

Kicking and screaming, Ezekiel was taken away from that place by the Spirit in the conveyance that had brought God to Ezekiel. He was an embittered and angry prophet (3:12-14), however, the hand (Spirit) of the Lord was strong upon him in this new location.

Ezekiel's Hesitant Obedience Ezekiel 3:15

Ezekiel obeyed the instructions of the Lord and went to the ghetto of the exiles living beside the river Chebar in Telabib. When he arrived he just sat in their midst for seven days without saying a word. This strange behavior is subject to several interpretations.

#1. Because of his embittered rage (3:14) he may have been sulking, perhaps staging a mild protest against this undesirable assignment.

#2. He may have been silent because he had heard nothing from the Lord during those seven days.

#3. Seven days is the normal period of mourning for the dead (Gen. 50:10; Num. 19:11; Job 2:13). Was he bearing silent witness to their spiritually dead state?

#4. This may be Ezekiel's seven day period of consecration as required for a priest's ordination (Lev. 8:33-36).

Whatever the reason for his silence he got their attention and irritated them by his behavior. One can imagine the questions they were probably asking. Who is he? What is he doing here? Why doesn't he speak? Possibly they knew him to be a prophet and had expected and then were disappointed that they were not hearing from the Lord.

His Mission Ezekiel 3:16-21

After the seven days of silence, during which his enraged spirit probably cooled down and he was more ready to listen, the word of the Lord came to him and further defined his call and mission. He was to be a WATCHMAN over the house of Israel.

Prophecies Prior To The Fall Of Jerusalem
Ezekiel 4-31 (minus 29:17-30:19)

The average Christian does not often turn to Ezekiel for his casual and devotional reading of the Scriptures nor for serious study. It is too much like the Revelation with strange visions and too much symbolism to handle well.

It is my intention to expose the reader to the time references and the structure of the book and thereby to determine which prophecies have already been fulfilled and which may pertain to what is commonly called the end times.

The Great Divide of the Book

The fall of Jerusalem to Nebuchadnezzar in 586 BC marks the dividing point of the two major divisions of the book.

Chapters 4-31 contain prophecies given to Ezekiel before the fall of Jerusalem and they pertain to that anticipated fall. These prophecies for the most part have already been fulfilled.

Chapters 32-48 present prophecies delivered after the fall of Jerusalem and may have some, but not necessarily all, prophecies that are yet to be fulfilled.

The Message Ezekiel Must Deliver Ezekiel 3:22-5:17

The same strong *"hand (Spirit) of the Lord"* that motivated Ezekiel to go to the exiles at Telabib (Eze. 3:14-15) now instructed him to leave them and to go to the plain where God had something more to tell him. Ezekiel got up and departed to that appointed place. When he arrived he was surprised that God had preceded him and was there in the same form and conveyance in which He had originally appeared as was recorded in 1:4-28 (Ezek. 3:23).

Amidst intriguingly strange instructions and activities God presented to Ezekiel the message that he was to deliver to the exiled nation. The main point of three dramatic object lessons was that Jerusalem will be put under a seige (4:1-8) which will produce famine (4:9-17). Chapters four and five sum up the end result—one third will die by the plague of fire and famine (4:17; 5:2, 4, 10, 12, 16, 17); one third will fall by the sword (4:2, 12, 17); one third will be scattered and exiled among the nations (4:13; 5:2, 10, 12, 14, 15).

The Time is Near Ezekiel 12:21-28

Ezekiel was called to his prophetic ministry around 592 BC, five years after being deported with Jehoiachin and others to Babylon in 597 BC. Thus the first six years of his prophetic ministry occurred prior to the fall and destruction of Jerusalem. Chapters 4-31 contain prophecies that pertained to that event.

Chapter twelve reveals that Israel was complaining that the divine prophecies (visions) were not being fulfilled. God told Ezekiel to tell Israel that *"the days draw near as well as the fulfillment of every vision"* that had been presented thus far. *"In your days"* what was spoken by Him through Ezekiel was to be performed. Israel was saying, *"the vision... is for many years from now, and he (Ezekiel) prophesies of times far off."* God said, *"None of My words will be delayed any longer."*

Therefore, we are assured that the prophecies given in chapters 4-31 before Jerusalem's fall were fulfilled in that generation to whom Ezekiel spoke. That being the case we turn now to the remainder of the book.

Prophecies After the Fall of Jerusalem
Ezekiel 32-48 (plus 29:17—30:19)

Chronologically chapter 32 does not immediately follow chapter 31. The starting point for the prophecies given after the fall of Jerusalem is at 33:21. Chronologically this latter half of the book should be read in this order: Ezekiel 33:21-39:29; 32:1-33:20; 40:1-48:35). After almost another two years he received his final revelation (29:17-30:19).

Three major subjects are dealt with in the latter part of the book: The restoration of Israel (Chapters 32-37); the wars of Gog and Magog (Chapters 38-39) and the blueprints of the proposed temple (Chapters 40-48).

The Restoration of Israel Chapters 32-37

Any study of the restoration of Israel should begin with Isaiah chapters ten and eleven. These chapters establish two important facts.

Two restorations of Israel are prophesied in the Scriptures. One must discern whether a particular restoration text pertains to the first (which is past) or the second (which is future) restoration.

The second restoration will occur after the return of Christ not as a sign preceding that event. Notice the progression of events. Isaiah 10:20-23 pertains to the first restoration; Isaiah 11:1-2 pertains to the incarnation; Isaiah 11:3-16 pertains to the second coming and Isaiah 11:11f pertains to the second restoration.

The Second Restoration Ezekiel 34:11-31

Three important facts are revealed concerning this future restoration.

#1. God Himself will be responsible for seeking out and delivering His scattered sheep to their own land. He will not search for and bring all biological Jews, but only those who are His sheep, those who exhibit faith in their Messiah,

Jesus. Verses 16, 17, 20 and 22 clearly indicate a selective and conditional regathering (Ezekiel 34:11-16 & 22).

#2. Israel will be under a covenant of peace; she will no longer be a prey (34:22, 28) or have reason to fear again (34:28). The harmful beasts (kings & nations) and their insults will be eliminated as they live securely.

#3. This will be a final and permanent restoration (34:22-29). It will occur after the return of Jesus. God will set over them His servant David as their sole shepherd. Some believe that the original David will be resurrected to rule over restored Israel. However, it is more in keeping with the teaching of the New Testament to understand this as a reference to Jesus who was promised that He would sit on the throne of David. On the day of Pentecost Peter preached that Jesus would fulfill that promise (Acts 2:30).

Ezekiel Chapters 36 and 37

It is difficult to discern with absolute certainty whether these two chapters pertain to the first or second restoration. In 36:8 and 22 it is said that this promise would soon be fulfilled because God is about to act. Yet, other verses suggest a permanency that could only be true of the second restoration.

Chapter 37 reaffirms the major facts presented in chapter 34 about the second restoration—the cleansing of those returning (37:23), the everlasting covenant of peace (37:26) and one king on the throne (37:24-25).

It should be noted that the present state of Israel and the return of many Jews to their homeland does not fulfill this prophecy. They do not exhibit a vital and obedient faith in God let alone their acceptance of His Son, Jesus; they are not living securely in the land and Jesus has not yet returned.

The Gog and Magog Affair Chapters 38-39

I totally agree with Clarence E. Mason, Jr. who, when he was at the Philadelphia College of the Bible, wrote, "One thing is certain; no teacher should speak dogmatically on a prophecy like that of Gog and Magog in Ezekiel 38 and 39." Some reasons for caution and humility include the fact that one cannot identify with absolute certainty the original Gog and Magog nor can one identify with absolute certainty the time and place when the prophecy is supposed to be fulfilled.

I believe that chapter 38:1-6 and chapter 39:1-20 relate to the original Gog and that chapter 38:7-23 and possibly chapter 39:21-24 pertain to the latter years (38:8) and the last days (38:16) invasion.

The Original Gog Ezekiel 38:1-6

Magog settled in the coastlands after the flood (Gen. 10:5). Many place Magog in northern Armenia west of the Caspian Sea. Some believe that its a collective name for people in Media and the Caucasian Mountains. Dr. J. Barton Payne places it farther north of the Black Sea. The text places it in *"the remote parts of the north"* leading some scholars to identify it as Russia.

Prince...of Meshech and Tubal Ezekiel 38:2

It is still debated whether there are three places named Rosh, Meshech and Tubal or whether Rosh means chief and modifies prince. The text would then read, "The chief prince of Meshech and Tubal."

According to Josesphus and others, Magog, Meshech and Tubal refer to the Scythians who invaded Asia Minor in 630 BC. These were tribes from the north of the Caucasus Mountains, the name of which supposedly means "Gog's Fort."

Some believe that Gog refers to Gyges, a familiar Lydian ruler about 662 BC. Others view it as a common title for kings of that country as was Pharaoh for the kings in Egypt.

His Allies Ezekiel 38:4-6

Gog's allies were Persia which is modern Iran; Cush which most believe is Ethiopia although there is much support for the land west of the Persian Gulf which is now part of Saudi Arabia (Gen. 10:7). Put is Libya in north Africa; Gomer is north Turkey or the forerunners of Germany; Beth-Togarmah is believed to be northern Turkey (Armenia).

God's Control of Gog Ezekiel 38:1-6

God told Ezekiel that He was about to yank the chain (take control) of Gog and his allies to reverse their good fortune and lead them to defeat and national ruin. That prophecy was fulfilled for it is noted that Meshech, Tubal and their multitude are in the pit of death which is Sheol (32:21-26). They have been slain by the sword which they had so freely wielded against others (32:26-28).

The Latter Day Gog Ezekiel 38:7-23

Do not over look the change in the time and subject that is noted in Ezekiel 38:8. What follows pertains to *"the latter years"* and *"the last days."* At that time another Gog will be summoned to come upon the land of Israel. He will be defeated and destroyed as was the original Gog (38:1-6 and 32:26-28). This invasion will take place after the second restoration (38:8, 12) during a time when Israel is secure (38:8, 11, 14) and prosperous (38:12-13) and after the Lord has returned (34:23f & Is. 11:3-16). It seems most likely that Revelation 20:9-10 identifies this invasion which will occur at the end of the millennial reign of Christ on earth as the final judgment begins.

The Invasion

God will initiate and control the affair by releasing Satan from his thousand years imprisonment (Rev. 20:7). Satan will then *"deceive the nations (Rev. 20:8)"* and, thus, *"the nations which are in the four corners of the earth (Rev. 20:8)"* numbered like the sand of the seashore will be gathered for the war.

While the size and strength of the assembled armies will seem invincible to themselves, God will respond with great fury as He orders a *"great earthquake in the land of Israel (Ezek. 38:199-20),"* also a sword (38:21) and pestilence (38:22) and a torrential rain with hail, fire and brimstone.

Final Judgment

All the texts support the idea that this is the beginning of the final judgment. In Ezekiel 38:22 God said, *"I will enter into judgment with him."* Revelation 20:11 immediately follows a description of this Gog and Magog affair with details of the final judgment.

Blueprints of the Proposed Temple Chapters 40-48

For 12 or 13 years Ezekiel had no known revelations from the Lord. Then in 572 BC, which was the 25th year of the exile and 14 years after Jerusalem had fallen, the Spirit of the Lord took him on a visionary trip to the land of Israel where he saw a structure like a city. The Spirit took him to that city where he saw a man who was to be his guide.

Ezekiel was instructed to carefully note everything that he saw and heard so that he could accurately report the same to the exiles. *"Declare to the house of Israel all that you see (Ezek. 40:4)."* It is evident and dare not be forgotten that this vision was for the benefit of the exiles and pertained to that time and circumstances. **THERE IS NOTHING IN CHAPTERS 40-48 THAT SUGGESTS THAT THIS VISION IS A PROPHECY THAT IS YET TO BE FULFILLED!**

Ezekiel was given the measurements and the lay-out of a proposed new temple that was to be built in his lifetime. Four viewpoints are taught regarding that temple.

#1. <u>The Temple Was Built</u>

Some believe that the temple was essentially built by the exiles upon their return from Babylon. However, that temple was so far from exact compliance to the blueprint given to Ezekiel that it seems very unlikely to have fulfilled this vision.

#2. <u>An Idealistic Vision</u>

Others believe that it was never intended to be built. Supposedly, it was Ezekiel's faith-wish that he might preach to the exiles and thereby give them something to hope for.

#3. <u>An Allegory</u>

Still others view this as an allegory which was meant to depict the grandeur and operation of the church.

#4. <u>The Millennial Temple</u>

A very popular view is that this is the blueprint for the temple that is supposedly to be built in Jerusalem when Israel is fully and finally restored. It is to serve all mankind during the millennial reign of Christ. The major problem with this view is that it is a mere assumption. There is nothing in the text that even suggests that it pertains to a future millennium.

I personally do not believe that any of these four views are correct.

Intended for Ezekiel's Contemporaries

Chapter 43 records the Lord's fourth visitation with Ezekiel. He came personally to reveal to Exekiel the purpose for this vision of the temple. God proposed that this temple could be His dwelling place among the restored Israelites, but the building of it and His dwelling among them was conditional. It was contingent upon their purity and faithfulness. *"Now let them put away their harlotry...far from Me; and I will dwell among them forever" (Ezek. 43:6-9).* It was also contingent upon their humility and willingness to build (Ezek. 43:10-12).

Ezekiel was told to describe the proposed temple to the house of Israel with the hope that they would be ashamed of their past and present iniquities. They were to measure or evaluate the proposed plans. <u>IF</u> they showed a repentant attitude and an eagerness to build the house so that God may dwell among them, <u>THEN</u> Ezekiel was to write out the plans in full detail before them so that they would build it and once again keep the statutes and the laws of God.

The Temple Was Never Built

There is no record or acknowledgment that they responded appropriately and met the conditions necessary for the building of that temple. It was never built nor was there any instruction or indication that it was meant to be built in the future.

This vision and these plans were for Ezekiel and the exiles to whom he ministered. This is certified by the specific instructions given in 43:20-27 that clearly indicates that Ezekiel himself was to be involved in the service within the proposed temple.

Those who eagerly teach that this is the millennial temple must tell us where in the Ezekiel text that is affirmed.

Ezekiel does not add much to our knowledge of the future. His prophecies in chapters 4-31 were fulfilled in the overthrow of Jerusalem and subsequent Babylonian captivity.

In chapters 32-48 some prophecies relative to the possible restoration of Israel and the final battle with the forces of Satan (Gog, Rev. 20) may await a future fulfillment, but the rebuilding of the temple pertained to Ezekiel's lifetime and has no relevance to our future.

CHAPTER NINE

THE CHURCH IN THE REVELATION

If one does not perceive that the Revelation is written to, for and about the church, which the Lamb, Jesus, *"purchased for God with His blood from every tribe and tongue and people and nation,"* he will miss the whole powerful point of this unveiling of divine truth about the future.

The Apocalypse is a prophetic (Rev. 1:3) revelation pertaining to the birth (Rev. 5:9-10), the purpose (1:6, 12; 5:10), the tribulated history (1:9; 4:1; 6:1-22:5) and the final glorified state of the church (2:7, 11; 3:5, 12; 20:6 & 21:1-22:5).

The centrality of the church as the subject and audience of the Revelation is evident in the introduction (1:1, 4, 11, 20), in the letters to the seven representative Asian churches (2:1, 8, 12, 18; 3:1, 7, 14) and repeated and reaffirmed in the epilogue (22:6, 16, 17).

The Church Identified as Individual Bondservants
Revelation 1:1-3

The Revelation was given for the benefit of the individual *bondservants* who collectively make up the church of Jesus

Christ. The term *doulos* identifies one who has voluntarily chosen to be a lifelong servant to his master. They are further defined as those whom Christ in His love has released from their sins and collectively made into a kingdom and made to be priests to His God and Father (1:5-6).

This Revelation is, then, an authoritative divine briefing from the Head of the church to its individual members concerning its immediate and continuing future.

The Church Functions in Local Assemblies
Revelation 1:4

The individual bondservant cannot prosper and grow and endure in isolation. He is, in his capacity as a bondservant of Jesus, a part of a kingdom who functions in cooperation with and complemented by his fellow priests in a local assembly. Hence, the Revelation will reach him through John's letters to the seven local congregations selected from among other congregations in Asia. Jesus selected these seven who are named because He had a specific word for each of them and collectively they represented the church universal. In apocalyptic literature the number seven often identifies that which is complete, the whole of something. Thus, at the conclusion of each letter to these churches, following the specific message to the local congregations, will be a challenge given by the Spirit to the individual member of the universal church—*"He who has an ear, let him hear what the Spirit says to the churches."*

The Plight of the Churches: "In the tribulation"
John writes as a brother and fellow partaker with those who, being, in the kingdom of Christ, are also *"in the tribulation"* that is the common lot of those who are *"in Jesus"* (Rev. 1:9). This is what necessitated and motivated God to communicate this Revelation to His church.

As we wrote in chapter four, Jesus and Paul both forewarned us that those who were *"in Christ"* were to expect to be in tribulation. Great tribulation began for the church with the stoning of Stephen (Acts 8:1 & 11:19) and continues throughout the whole present church age.

The Desire & Need of the Church:
"Grace to you & peace."

The churches, being in tribulation and anticipating increasingly difficult times, needed and desired to live in peace. They would only experience that as God's abundant and timely grace would equip them to endure *"the things soon to take place" (Rev. 1:1-2)* and *"the things that will take place (later) after these things" (Rev. 4:1)*. There is no other road to peace except by the grace of God.

While peace-producing grace will be supplied by God *"who is and who was and who is to come"* and from *"the seven Spirits who are before His throne"* it will mostly be channeled through the Lord Jesus Christ through His faithful witness as He communicates and implements this accurate, authoritative prophecy which He delivers unchanged from the mind and heart of God. Being the first-born of the dead He ever liveth to administer the necessary grace to every generation of believers; and by that designation there is conveyed the promise that others will follow, that death and the grave will not be the destiny of those who are in Jesus. His followers need not fear death for He has seized the keys and taken control over death and Hades.

Present grace was needed and supplied by Jesus as the ruler of the kings of the earth in order to endure the Roman Emperors who were responsible for much of the church's tribulation.

The Hope of the Church: "Behold, He is coming"

John gets very excited as he contemplates what Christ has done for the church. He is impelled to pronounce a benediction of praise upon Him. *"To Him be the glory and the dominion for ever and ever. Amen" (Rev. 1:6).*

#1. Because He loves us. The verb is in the present tense. We know He loved us in the past for *"Greater love has no man than this, that one lay down his life for his friends" (John 15:13).* Paul bore a similar witness, *"Christ also loved the church and gave Himself up for her" (Eph. 5:25).* Now we are assured of His continuing present love as He pours out His Spirit upon us and intercedes before the throne of God on our behalf to maintain our faith and place in the family of God.

#2. Because He released us from our sins. God has already judged the whole human race. His verdict is that *"all have sinned and fall short"* of His glory (Rom. 3:23) and *"There is none righteous, not even one" (Rom. 3:9).*

Further, the sentence has already been pronounced for all who have sinned. *"The soul who sins will die" (Ezek. 18:4)* for *"The wages of sin is death" (Rom. 6:23).*

Therefore, a sense of great relief and heartfelt gratitude prevails as John reflects upon the power of the gospel and the amazing grace of our God and His Christ for He has not dealt with us according to our sins, but has pardoned and *"released us from our sins."*

#3. Because He made us to be a kingdom. Those whom Christ has purchased by His blood have become His kingdom, a kingdom of priests intended to serve God and eventually reign upon the earth (Rev. 5:10; Dan. 7:18, 22). It will be a kingdom not defined by geographical boundaries or race but by faith in the Lord Jesus Christ.

With great, almost uncontrollable emotion, John blurts out ecstatically, *"Behold, He is coming;"* this one of whom we are speaking in glowing terms; the one and only Lord

Jesus Christ whom death could not hold and kings cannot subdue is going to return. When He does *"every eye will see Him"* and He will reign until *"...every created thing which is in heaven and on the earth and under the earth and on the sea, and all things in them"* will say *"To Him who sits on the throne, and to the Lamb, be blessing and honor and glory and dominion forever and ever"* (Rev. 5:13).

Jesus Walks Among His Churches
Revelation 1:12-3:22

In this first vision in the Revelation the resurrected and living Jesus appeared to John while he was in the Spirit. The point of the vision being that Jesus was already actively present among the seven Asian churches which, by the symbolic number seven, represented the universal church. As the Head of the church He is constantly present to evaluate the local church and advise it to hold to the doctrinal and behavioral standards which He requires for their continuance.

He manifests and maintains control of each local church through its leaders (stars) which He holds in His right hand. He supports, strengthens and guides them, but also holds them responsible and accountable for the state of the churches they oversee.

Jesus Speaks to the Local Churches

The very first words that He has for John, which would surely be passed on to the whole church, was, *"Do not be afraid..."* (Rev. 1:17). Whatever tribulation the church may face, even if it includes the martyrdom of many, the living One who is alive forever and possesses the keys to death and Hades will see to it that, as He promised from the beginning, *"the gates of Hades shall not over power it"* (Mt. 16:18).

After making an inspection tour of each church He reported to them their strengths and their weaknesses and what they must do to persevere and be ready for His ultimate return.

The details given in each letter pertain to that particular congregation and the time of its existence. Except by way of example, they have no hearing on the future history of the universal church; they do not represent chronological periods of church history.

The Holy Spirit Speaks to the Universal Church

Each letter which Jesus had dictated to John concluded with a message from the Holy Spirit for all the churches and individual believers of every generation and place. *"He who has an ear, let him hear what the Spirit says to the churches."*

The Spirit's sevenfold challenge and encouragement to the church is that each one be an *overcomer*. The verb is *nikao* which elsewhere (Rev. 6:2) is translated *conquer*. An overcomer (conqueror) is one who persists in the faith, enduring whatever trials and tribulations he may encounter while faithfully participating in the spread of the gospel and the upbuilding of the kingdom of Christ which is the church.

The Spirit promises great blessings to those who overcome. Most of the promised blessings to overcomers pertain to and will be fulfilled either in the millennium or in the eternal state of the church. Overcomers will have access to the tree of life in the Paradise of God (Rev. 2:7; 22:2, 22); they will not be hurt by the second death (Hell, Rev. 2:11; 20:14); they will receive hidden manna for sustenance during times of scarcity and a white stone (a positive vote for life) with a new name on it (Rev. 2:17). They will exercise ruling authority over the nations (Rev. 2:26-27) and be given the morning star (2:28). They will be dressed in white garments of righteousness and not have their names erased from the book of life (Rev. 3:5; 20:15). They will be pillars in the temple of God and registered for residence in the new Jerusalem (Rev. 3:12; 21:2, 10-22:5) and they shall sit down with Christ on the throne of God (Rev. 3:21).

The Purchase & Purpose of the Church
Revelation 4:1-5:14

The same voice which ordered John to write his visions in a book now invited him to visit heaven in the Spirit. The stated purpose for the visit was to show him things that must take place in the future.

Pretribulational Deception

Pretribulational teachers affirm that the rapture occurs at this point (4:1) in the Revelation. What utter nonsense! There is not the slightest hint of the return of Christ and the rapture at this juncture in the Revelation. Revelation 4:1 only describes the circumstances under which John visited heaven and received a revelation of the tribulated history and future of the church.

Intelligent and honest pretribbers must be embarrassed and suppress a twinge of guilt when they or their fellow pretribbers impose the rapture on the Revelation at this point. They embarrass themselves still further by offering as proof for the rapture occurring at Revelation 4:1 the ludicrous supposition that the church is not mentioned in chapters 4-19. Anyone who cannot see the church in chapters 4-19 is reading the Revelation wearing self-imposed blinders. One constantly encounters the church throughout the Revelation.

The Birth of the Church Revelation 5:9-10

Upon his entrance into heaven John is dazzled by the sight of the heavenly throne, the One sitting upon it and the constant worship of God by the inhabitants of heaven (Rev. 4).

In a flashback vision he then witnesses the slain Lamb's return to heaven on the day of His resurrection (Rev. 5:6f). All of heaven celebrated the birth of the church by the slain Lamb. *"Thou wast slain and didst purchase for God with Thy blood men from every tribe and tongue and people and nation."* The church is then identified as *"a kingdom and priests to our God"* and promised that *"they will reign upon the earth" (Rev. 5:9-10 & 1:5-6).*

The Tribulated History of the Church
Revelation 6:1-9:21

When Jesus opened the first of seven seals a white horse rider appeared who went out conquering (overcoming) and to conquer (overcome).

How do we determine who the white horse rider represented? We dare not arbitrarily assign an identification. We are dependent upon the text. What has the text presented thus far in the Revelation that will identify this rider? The Revelation textual evidence overwhelmingly presents the church as the white horse rider for the following reasons.

#1. The Revelation was written to and about the church.

As stated earlier, the apocalypse is a prophetic (1:3) revelation of the birth (1:5, 5:9), purpose (1:6; 5:10) and tribulated history (1:9, 4:1; 6:1-22:5) of the church. It follows naturally that the opening of the seals may relate to the affairs or history of the church.

#2. The Spirit issued seven calls for the church to overcome.

The concluding word of the Spirit to the church in each of the seven letters was a promise of great blessings if the church would overcome. The word is *nikao* which in 6:2 is translated *conquer*. Seven times the call goes forth, conquer — conquer — conquer — conquer — conquer —

conquer—conquer! Thus in Revelation 6:1-2 John sees the church going forth in obedience to the great commission *"to make disciples of all the nations (Mt. 28:19)"* having been empowered by the Holy Spirit to be Christ's witnesses *"to the remotest part of the earth (Acts 1:8)."*

#3. The Color White

Colors were assigned by God and intentionally given to depict the character and nature of each rider. Already five white things have been identified in the Revelation and they are presented as righteous or heavenly persons or things (Rev. 1:14, 2:17; 3:4-5, 18 & 4:4). It is not without significance that later the saints will be seen clothed in white linen and riding on white horses (Rev. 19:14).

#4. A Kingdom of Priests

In the continuity of the text, which is always important, just before the white horse rider goes forth, the church is purposefully acknowledged to be a kingdom with the promise that they shall reign on the earth. They are appropriately given a crown and sent forth conquering and to conquer (Rev. 6:1-2).

#5. The Fifth Seal Factor

There is a repeated pattern in each of the series of seven seals, trumpets and bowls. The first four in each series are a closely related cluster of similar symbols or events while the fifth of each series identifies the group that is featured or targeted in that series.

The fifth bowl identifies the kingdom of the beast as the object of the bowls of wrath (Rev. 16:10).

The fifth trumpet depicts locusts that attack only those not sealed by God (Rev. 9:4), thereby identifying the worshippers of the beast as the target of the trumpeted events.

Similarly, the fifth seal features the martyrdom of the saints and identifies them as the subject of the seals series.

Not The Beast (Antichrist)
The popular pretribulationalist teaching is that the white horse rider is the antichrist. But there is no textual support for that identification, absolutely none! The antichrist or beast has not yet been introduced into the Revelation and does not appear until 11:7 and again in chapter 13. At this point in the Revelation (6:1-2) there is nothing to suggest or warrant the identification of the antichrist as the white horse rider. Pretribulationalists simply arbitrarily announce that identification.

The World the Church Encounters Revelation 6:3-8
The seven seals reveal the tribulated history of the church in the world it seeks to conquer. Having referenced its birth and purpose in 5:9-10 the seals foretell the time period from the beginning of its evangelistic mission (Rev. 6:1-2) to the end of the age when the cosmic signs will signal the soon return of Christ (Rev. 6:12-11:15).

The church and the world will encounter the red horse of war (Rev. 6:3-4), the black horse of famine (Rev. 6:5-6), and the ashen horse of pestilence and wild beasts (evil kings)—all of which will bring a fourth of the earth to death and Hades (Rev. 6:7-8).

The church will not be exempt from the ravages of war, famine, pestilence and evil rulers. In addition, some of those who go forth conquering and to conquer (Rev. 6:2) will be killed *"because of the Word of God, and because of the testimony they had maintained" (Rev. 6:9)*. In heaven those martyrs cry out for judgment against those responsible for their deaths.

The Church in the End Times
Revelation 6:12—11:13

The martyrs in heaven are told that they must rest and wait for the *"judging and avenging"* of their deaths until the number of martyrs and the number of their fellow believers is complete (Rev. 6:11). Seals #6 and 7 (7 trumpets) cover the end times when the church of this age will be completed; the fullness of the Gentiles will have come in (Rom. 11:25).

Before the church is completed there will be cosmic signs that will signal the approaching end of the church's tribulation and the nearness of Christ's return. The signs will be a world-wide earthquake (Rev. 6:12) and a shaking of the powers of the heavens (Rev. 6:13-15; Mt. 24:29).

The Sealing of the Church Revelation 7:1-17

To be sealed is to be branded as belonging to God and being under His divine protection and grace.

The term bondservants always identifies believers in the Lord Jesus Christ who comprise the church. They are identified as Jewish believers because in its infancy the church was almost totally Jewish.

The 144,000, being a very large round number and a multiple of 12, which is the number of the church, must not necessarily be taken literally. It is a symbolical number representing the whole church at the time the Revelation was given. It represents the apostolic Jewish church, the church in its infancy, the first fruits purchased by the blood of Christ (Rev. 14:4 & James 1:18).

John was then given a vision of the completed church, the universal church from every nation, tribes, peoples and tongues. They came out of the great tribulation of this present age (Rev. 7:14; 6:1-7:10). The 144,000 are the first fruits (Rev. 4:14 & James 1:18). The great multitude are the full fruits, the church in its maturity and completion.

The Prayers of the Church Revelation 8:1-9:21

Throughout the New Testament the term saints is clearly and consistently used to refer to the people of God, Christian believers, the called out church of the Lord Jesus.

In response to the prayers of the saints (Rev. 8:1-5) God will send six trumpeted catastrophes upon the earth in an attempt to bring men to repentance before the Lord returns. Many will be killed but those who are spared will continue in their hardened sinful conduct (Rev. 9:20-21). The church may then be under the supernatural protection of God as in the case of the locust plague when only those not sealed by God will be harmed.

The Measurement of the Church Revelation 10:1-11:2

After the seventh seal is broken (Rev. 8:11) and the six trumpeted events are past, a strong angel (10:1) appears to John to announce that *"there shall be delay no longer...the mystery (unveiled plan) of God is finished" (Rev. 10:6-7).* The church will be complete and the Lord will return; at which time the resurrection and rapture will occur.

John is asked to measure the temple, those who worship in it (Rev. 11:1-2). It was not a literal temple John was to measure. He was on the isle of Patmos far removed from the temple site; and the temple, having been destroyed in AD 70, was no longer in existence to be measured. The temple represents true Israel, the remnant who believe in the Lord Jesus. Individual Christians are acknowledged to be temples of God (I Cor. 3:16-17) and collectively the church is the temple of the living God (II Cor. 6:16; Eph. 2:31 and Rom. 11:25).

Why does one measure anything? To determine that it is the right size or quantity; the intended size and quantity. We measure things to determine if they are full, complete or finished. By measuring we check the progress or readiness of things in order to proceed to the next step or make necessary alterations in one's project or mission. John is to measure the church so as to be assured and to confirm that the church is complete and the time is right for the finishing of the mystery of God (Rev. 10:7) and the return of Christ.

The Church Under the Beast in the Last Days
Revelation 11:3-13; 12:1-3:18; 17:1-19:10

Although there will be wide-spread apostasy in the latter days, the true church will be very strong and possessed with holy boldness.

The Lord's Two Prophets Revelation 11:3-13

This bold strength will be in evidence by the prophetic ministry of two Spirit-filled men who in turn will encourage and inspire others to be faithful and true.

The strength and strong witness of the church will be seen when these two are finally killed by the beast. Their burial is delayed for three and a half days by the long line of Christians who view their bodies. Verse 10 describes the reaction of the Christian community to their martyrdom. The idiomatic phrase *"those from the peoples and tribes and tongues and nations"* always identifies the church while the idiomatic phrase in verse 11 *"those who dwell on the earth"* refers to the reaction of the unbelieving world.

Satan's Two Prophets Revelation 12:1-13:18

John was taken back in a vision to the birth (12:1-4) and the ascension of Jesus (12:5) in order to show why and how the church came under tribulation. After Jesus' ascension (12:5) there was war in heaven (12:7) which resulted in Satan being cast out of heaven into the earth (12:9-12). In great anger Satan persecuted Israel (12:13-17) and then also the church, those *"who keep the commandment of God and hold to the testimony of Jesus" (12:17).*

Acts 8:1 coupled with 11:19 reveal that the great persecution (8:1) or tribulation (thilpsis in Acts 11:19) of the church began with the stoning of Stephen.

Scripture, as well as history, records that it has continued periodically from time to time and place to place throughout this age.

Chapter thirteen focuses on the continuing tribulation of the church in the last 42 months of its tribulated history. Satan will empower a beastly king and a false prophet who will *"make war with the saints and overcome them" (Rev. 13:7).*

The Church Called to Sanctification Before Babylon Falls
Revelation 17-18

The harlot city (17:1) whose code name is Babylon the Great (17:5) will be responsible for much immorality, ungodliness and the martyrdom of Christians (Rev. 17:6; 18:20, 24 & 19:2). Therefore she will be judged (17:1) and suffer a fiery destruction (18:8, 9, 17, 18) at the hands of the beast and ten allies (17:11-12, 16-17).

An angelic voice (possibly the same one who will preach the gospel Rev. 14:9-12) will call the church to separate from the harlot so as not to participate in her sins and her judgment (18:4-8).

Revelation 19:1-6 records the celebration in heaven that occurs after mystery Babylon's fall.

The Church, as the Bride, is Ready for Her Wedding—
The Rapture

"Let us rejoice and be glad and give the glory to Him, for the marriage of the Lamb has come and His bride has made herself ready" (Rev. 19:7). The next verse identifies the saints as the bride. It is generally agreed upon by pre-mid-post-tribulationalists that the church is the bride of Christ. In John 3:20 Jesus alluded to Himself as a bridegroom and His

followers as the bride. In Matthew 25:1, 6 and 10 He alluded to His coming as a bridegroom for His bride. Jewish and Gentile Christians (Rom. 7:4) are betrothed to Christ (II Cor. 11:2) with the actual marriage to take place at His coming.

It is thought by many (including pretribbers) that, with the marriage taking place at the rapture, the wedding feast represents the millennial reign of Christ after which He will take His bride (new Jerusalem, the church) to their home, the new heaven and earth, where they will live together forever (Rev. 21-22).

The Return of Christ Revelation 1:7; 11:15-19

The Second Coming of Christ is introduced early in the Revelation (1:7) as the climactic keystone event of the future and as the great hope and longing of the Christian church. Yet the point at which it occurs in the chronology of the Revelation is never simply and clearly stated nor is that event ever described. However, since the sounding of the seventh trumpet calls for a celebration of the beginning of His reign over the kingdom of the world, it must be assumed that He has come at this point. On the basis of I Corinthians 15:52 and I Thessalonians 4:16 it is probably to be assumed that His coming occurs at the beginning of the seventh trumpet period.

Revelation 11:18-19 provides a summary or index of several major events that will occur during that lengthy period after the return of Christ.

The Church
After the Second Coming Revelation 14:1f

Having been transformed (I Cor. 15:52), raptured to meet the coming Lord in the air (I Thess. 4:16) and accompanying Him in His decent to the earth, the church is subsequently seen with Him on Mt. Zion (Rev. 14:1) as represented by the 144,000.

The 144,000 were introduced in Revelation 7:1-8 as the first fruits of the Lamb's sacrificial death (Rev. 14:5; James 2:18), symbolically representing the infant Jewish church. Throughout this age the 144,00 infant church will have grown into a great multitude that no man can number (Rev. 7:9-17). The identification of the 144,000 with the entire church is confirmed in Revelation 17:14 where those who are with Him are *"the called and chosen and faithful"* which most certainly describes the persevering and overcoming church.

Second Advent Converts Revelation 14:6-16; 15:2-11

After the return of Jesus many will be added to the church and become a part of the eventual great multitude that cannot be numbered (Rev. 7:9-17). This will occur when three angels preach the gospel from mid-heaven (14:6-11) in addition to the personal witness of Jesus (19:15) and the priestly ministry of the glorified saints.

Many of them may *"die in the Lord"* at the hands of the beast (13:7, 15) prior to his destruction at Armageddon. In a continuing vision John saw them standing before God having *"come off victorious from the beast and from the image of his name" (Rev. 15:2)*.

Victorious at Armageddon

It is foretold that ten kings and their armies will ally themselves with the beasts to wage war against the Lamb who is the Lord of lords and the King of kings. And the church will be with Him for that war (Rev. 17:14).

So, then, when the Euphrates River dries up and the kings of the earth gather at Armageddon (Rev. 16:16) they will assemble with the specific purpose of warring against the King of kings and Lord of lords upon His white horse (19:11, 16, 19) and against His army (19:19).

Reigning In The Millennium

Jesus promised to *"give authority over the nations" (Rev. 2:26)* to those who overcome while He rules them with a rod of iron. Later He said that they would *"sit down with Me on My throne" (Rev. 3:21)* meaning that they would reign with Him. When the creatures of heaven celebrated the purchase of the church by Jesus' shed blood it was clearly forecast that the church would *"reign upon the earth" (5:10)*.

Their reign shall extend into their eternal habitation in the new heaven and earth where they will serve God and the Lamb and *"reign forever and ever" (Rev. 22:5)*.

The Eternal State of the Church Revelation 21-22

The church, which is the bride of Christ (Rev. 19:7-8), is also described as the new Jerusalem (Rev. 21:2, 9). After the great white thrown judgment (Rev. 20:11) and the replacement of the first heaven and earth with a new heaven and earth (Rev. 20:11, 21:1 and I Pet. 3:10-13) the church will come down from heaven to settle upon the perfect earth where God will live among them forever. There they will eternally *"eat of the tree of life—the Lord Jesus" (Rev. 2:7; 22:1)* and drink of the *"river of the water of life—the Holy Spirit" (Rev. 22:1);* and God will be living with them forever (Rev. 21:3-4).

The Revelation is best understood if we allow it to tell its own story by interpreting all of its parts by the surrounding contexts. To force the rapture into it at 4:1 and by naming the antichrist as the white horse rider at 6:2, pretribulationalists present a warped and self-determined interpretation of this marvelous book.

And while Israel may not be totally out of the picture, it is the church which is the focus of the Revelation and the glorious future which God is creating.

CHAPTER TEN

I WILL COME AGAIN
John 14:1-3

Along with Daniel 9:24-27 and Matthew 24:4-28 this passage is one of the most misunderstood and misappropriated passages in the Bible.

The King James version of the Bible, which many of us read as we grew up, unfortunately translated the Greek word *monai* as mansions and Stuart Hamblen inspired us all to sing along with him, "I've got a mansion just over the hilltop in that bright land where we'll never grow old." Thus like most Christians, including most preachers and prophecy teachers, we became confused, deceived and simply wrong about Jesus' promises found in John 14:1-3.

Two related reasons contribute to it being misunderstood. The first is the failure to study the larger context (John 13:1-17:26) and to allow it to clarify what Jesus meant by His promises. The second is the failure to perceive that these promises were given to a few designated people, His apostles, in a specific historical setting. It must be understood that these promises apply first of all to them and their situation. He was not making a general statement to and about the general public and certainly not to a future generation.

Three Erroneous Interpretations

There are three main interpretations given to these three verses with reference to their fulfillment.

#1. A Funeral Text

Dr. J. Barton Payne in his <u>Encyclopedia of Biblical Prophecy</u> writes that some believe that these verses must be understood as a promise that Jesus will come to take us to heaven when we die.

Most pastors must plead guilty to a practical acceptance of that interpretation since, along with Psalm 23, it is probably the most frequently read Scriptural text before and during funeral services.

This view must be rejected. Jesus was not talking about what happens at death. Death is not the occasion when Jesus returns to us and receives us to Himself. It is the occasion in which we go to Him. At death we shall experience the reality of II Corinthians 5:1-8 as we immediately shall be *"at home with the Lord."*

#2. The Coming of the Holy Spirit

A significant number of Bible students believe that Jesus fulfilled this promise in the Pentecostal outpouring of the Holy Spirit. While Jesus does also instruct and encourage His apostles about the coming of the Holy Spirit in this extended discourse, the Holy Spirit as a member of the Trinity was sent (John 14:16; 16:7) by Jesus and the Father while they remained in heaven. The Holy Spirit was *"<u>another</u> helper (paraclete)"* in addition to Jesus.

#3. A Rapture Text

The majority of Bible students wrongly understand this text to be a promise of a general rapture for all Christians living in some future generation.

The Second Coming of Christ is such a blessed hope and so eagerly anticipated that when Jesus says, *"I will come again"* many immediately and desirably assume that He must be referring to that momentous event. They do not bother to read the prior and following context for a fuller explanation of this promise or even consider the possibility that He could be referring to some other coming at another time.

While we must always guard against being too dogmatic in teaching prophecy, there are some things so plainly stated and obviously supported by the text that one can and should speak and write with great certainty and conviction about them. This is one such a text. Therefore I shall declare emphatically that, contrary to what is popularly taught and commonly understood, in John 14:1-3 Jesus has said absolutely nothing about His future return or the rapture. We shall endeavor to clearly support that conclusion when we study the text in its context.

This text is so vitally important to pretribulationalists in their vain effort to find and maintain some semblance of Scriptural support for their belief and teaching about the rapture that they simply dare not and will not allow themselves to consider alternate interpretations—no matter how convincing the evidence for the correctness of the alternate interpretation and the error of their own.

If one understands the historical context as intentionally presented in John 13:1-17: 26 and perceives that clearly Jesus made these promises to His twelve disciples then it will be evident and certain that John 14:1-3 contains promises made specifically and solely to His apostles to assure them that He would come back to them after His death and resurrection to receive them again.

The Time & Circumstance of Jesus' Promises

No text can be properly understood apart from its context. Almost everyone pays lip service to this principle, yet it is frequently disregarded by even the most popular and scholarly commentators, writers and teachers.

John 14:1-3 is a very small segment in a series of closely connected conversations which Jesus had with His apostles beginning at 13:1 and concluding at 17:26. John 13:1 sets forth the significant circumstances, purposes and motivation for this whole section of conversational teaching.

The Occasion: The Feast of Passover

It was prior to the Feast of Passover when this conversation began. At the feast every family would kill their best lamb to commemorate the exodus from Egypt and to atone for their sins.

This Feast of Passover would be different. God was going to slay a lamb, His best Lamb, His perfect Son, Jesus. This *"once and for all"* sacrifice of a totally innocent man would be an efficacious propitiation for the sins of the world and would enable men to be born of the Spirit into the household of God.

The Imminent Event: The Death of Jesus

All that Jesus spoke in this series of conversations was prompted by the fact that He knew *"that His hour had come that He should depart out of this world to the Father."* He knew that He was going to die and in that death He would *"depart out of this world"* and He would *"go to His Father."*

These chapters (13-17) are all about what will be accomplished by His departure out of the world to the Father and what will subsequently take place. His imminent crucifixion is the reason for this extended conversation with His apostles.

The Motivation: Love & Concern for His Apostles

"Having loved His own who were in the world, He loved them to the end."

Jesus purpose in this extended conversation (chapters 13-17) was to prepare His apostles for His death and to reassure them about their immediate future. The whole conversation was with and for the benefit of the apostles personally and specifically. These chapters do not contain general teaching spoken to and for the benefit of Israel or the multitude of disciples who followed Him; and it certainly was not directed to or for the benefit of the yet-to-be-born church.

This intent to enlighten and prepare the apostles for His departure, which is strongly noted in John 14:29; 15:17; 16:1-4; 16:25, 33 and chapter 17, is evident in the words with which He introduced His promises in 14:1-3, *"Let not your heart be troubled; you believe in God, believe also in Me."*

Jesus knew the turmoil and confusion building up within His apostles. He encouraged them not to be troubled or perplexed over His imminent death. He asked them to trust Him in what He is about to do and to believe all that He is telling them. This call to maintain their faith in Him is evident throughout this conversation.

In John 14:1-3 Jesus made two separate but related promises—to prepare a place for His disciples in His Father's house(hold) and to return to them after His departure.

Promise Number One John 14:2

"In My Father's house(hold) are many dwelling places;... I go (am going to die) to prepare a place for you (in My Father's household)."

Though seemingly *elementary*, in order to understand this and the second promise made in verse three it is absolutely necessary to answer the simple questions a good reporter asks in order to get the facts correct in an important story.

Who Made the Promise?

Who is the person speaking and making this promise? It is so obvious that we all agree and there is no controversy or debate over who was speaking. No one would dare to suggest that it was anyone but Jesus. He is named in John 13:38. If I, or anyone else, would foolishly suggest someone else we would be criticized and condemned and our interpretation rightly rejected.

To Whom Was the Promise Made?

Jesus was speaking face to face with Peter and the apostles when He said, *"Let not your heart be troubled...I go to prepare a place for you."*

Obviously, Jesus was speaking and making this promise to Peter (John 13:37) and the rest of the apostles (13:5, 22, 33, 35 and 14:5, 8 etc.). This was not spoken to the Jews in general, the nation of Israel. Nor was it said to any future generation. If we do not have the right or reason to identify the speaker, "I", as someone other than Jesus neither do we have the right or reason to identify the "you" to whom the promises are made as someone other than the apostles. Yet, Bible commentators, prophecy teachers, preachers and lay prophecy buffs, who would not think of changing the identity of the speaker—and who would strongly condemn anyone who did so—do not hesitate to change the identity of those to whom the promise was made by saying that the *"you"* refers to a generation of Christians to be born thousands of years later.

With reference to this promise to *"prepare a place"* for the apostles in the Father's house or household, two clarifying questions must be answered.

#1. What and Where is the Father's House?

The Greek word for *house* is *oikia* which can and sometimes does refer to a structure, an edifice. However, the word is also often used to refer to the residents of a house meaning, therefore, the household or family unit.

Joshua affirmed, *"But as for me and my house we will serve the Lord."* Was he committing his tent or building to the service of God? Of course not, we understand that he was talking about his household or family. *Oikia* has that meaning in Matthew 12:25, John 4:53, I Corinthians 16:15, Ephesians 2:19 and Philippians 4:22.

The Psalmist said, *"One thing I have asked of the Lord, that I shall seek; that I may dwell in the house of the Lord all the days of my life..."* Was he contemplating going to heaven to live in a cottage or a mansion there? Certainly not; he was asking to be able to dwell in God's house all the days of his life here on earth.

The Father's house is neither a building nor is it heaven. God does not dwell in a structure of any kind. He is omnipresent and fills all things and places. Solomon said that even the highest heaven cannot contain Him. While some texts do speak of heaven as God's dwelling place they never speak of it as His house. Jesus did not say, as we have been led to believe, *"In heaven there are many dwelling places."* In fact heaven is never mentioned in chapters 14-16. The point of this chapter and promise is not that He is going to heaven, but that He is going to His Father.

Hebrews 3:2-6 helps us to understand that God's house is not a building nor a dwelling place in heaven. The Father's house(hold) is the Christian Church comprised of His chosen and reborn children. Remnant Israel was called *"His house"* (God's household) over which Moses was responsible as God's servant. Then, as now, God's house was not in heaven but here on earth (Heb. 3:2, 5). Similarly, now Christ is God's servant as head *"over <u>His house</u> WHOSE HOUSE WE ARE!" (Heb. 3:6)*. There it is simply, plainly and conclusively stated — God's house is not a building or a place either in heaven or on earth; it is people, the family or household of God. One does not have to go to or be in heaven to be in the Father's house.

Paul confirms rather profusely that the church is the household of God in I Corinthians 3:9, 16; II Corinthians 6:16, 18; Ephesians 2:19-22 and most clearly in I Timothy where he wrote of *"the household of God, which is the church of the living God."*

#2. How Will Jesus "*Prepare A Place*" For His Disciples in the Father's Household?

Having been unduly influenced by the King James translation of *monai* as mansions we have wrongly conjured up a picture of Jesus constructing a heavenly building for us to dwell in.

The word simply means to make the necessary arrangements for whatever the occasion or need. It is used rather frequently in the New Testament to indicate the preparations or arrangements necessary for a meal, an anointing, a wedding, the arrival of an important person etc, but it is never used to indicate the building of an edifice. When Paul asked Philemon to *"prepare a lodging"* he was not asking him to erect a mansion or a cottage for him. He was only asking him to make the necessary arrangements for a place to stay and rest.

"I go to prepare a place for you..." The words have a deeper meaning than simply saying that He was to leave one place and go to another. They take us back to the introductory verse of this entire section (John 13:1-17:26) and the imminent event which motivated this whole conversation— *"His hour had come that He should depart out of this world to the Father."* When He said, *"I go"* He means, *"I am going to die (depart out of this world) in order to prepare a place for you in the Father's house(hold).*

In his popular song Stuart Hamblen has solidified the false notion, planted in our minds by the King James wrong rendition of *monai* as mansions, that Jesus went to heaven to build a "mansion just over the hilltop in that bright land where we'll never grow old." Unfortunately **THAT IS A TOTAL MISCONCEPTION!** There is not a verse or a suggestion anywhere in the Bible to the effect that Jesus is constructing or preparing a building for us in heaven.

The preparation of the place for the disciples in the Father's house was not to be accomplished when He gets to the Father, but by His going, that is, by His departure out of this world to the Father, i.e., His crucifixion.

How does one get into the Father's house(hold) and become a part of the family of God? He must be born into it. Jesus made possible that spiritual birth by His substitutionary and atoning death which provided the pardon for our sins. *"As many as received Him, to them He gave the right to become the children of God (John 1:12)."* Thus He died *"to prepare a place for you."*

The Second Promise John 14:3

"And if I go (depart out of the world to the Father) and prepare a place for you (in My Father's house), I will come again, and receive you (apostles) to Myself; that where I am (in My Father's house), there you may be also."

This promise has been generally misunderstood and misinterpreted (myself included until recent years) as a statement about the rapture. We ought to be ashamed for having missed the obvious meaning of it since Jesus spoke very plainly and explained in His continuing discourse that He was promising to come back to His apostles after His death and resurrection.

The reporter's questions that were asked in order to understand the first promise (vs. 2) apply to this second promise (vs. 3) also. Jesus was the one making the promise and He made it to His apostles. If we accept Jesus' words literally and in the context of John 13:1-17:26 this absolutely cannot be a promise of His future return or of the accompanying rapture.

Jesus States When the Promise Will Be Fulfilled

Many Bible students and especially prophecy teachers seem unaware that Jesus told us very plainly when this promise would be fulfilled. If everything I have written thus far about this promise is rejected as unconvincing, what follows should be sufficient in itself to convince everyone that Jesus' promise in John 14:1-3 pertained to His return to the apostles after the resurrection. Jesus said that His promise would be fulfilled *"AFTER A LITTLE WHILE."*

As He continued this conversation with His apostles, at least three times He gave expanded commentary on the promise given in 14:1-3. I berate myself for having missed these time statements all these years.

John 14:18-19

"*I will not leave you (apostles) as orphans, I will come to you (apostles).*" When? "*After a little while, the world will behold Me no more (because I'm going to die), but you (apostles) will behold Me!*"

John 14:28

"*You (apostles) heard that I said to you (in vss. 1-3), 'I go away, and I will come to you (apostles)'.*" He did not say anything about coming to a generation of believers two thousand or more years later.

John 16:16-22

"*A little while (2nd ref.), and you will no longer behold Me; and again a little while (3rd ref.), and you (apostles) will see Me (as promised in 14:1-3).*

Some of His disciples therefore said to one another, 'What is this thing He is telling us, a little while (4th ref.), and you will see Me, and because I go to the Father?'" The latter phrase is an obvious reference back to the original promise in 14:1-3.

"And so they were saying, 'What is this that He says, A little while (5th ref.)?' We do not know what He is talking about.

Jesus knew that they wished to question Him, and He said to them, 'Are you deliberating together about this, that I said, A little while (6th ref.), and you will not behold Me, and again a little while (7th ref.), and you will see Me? Truly, truly , I say to you, that you will weep and lament, but the world will rejoice (when I die); you will be sorrowful, but your sorrow will be turned to joy. (Verse 21 is omitted). Therefore you, too, now have sorrow; but I will see you again, and no one takes your joy away from you.'"

Fulfilled: Post-Resurrection Appearances

The *"little while"* which Jesus said would pass until this promise would be fulfilled cannot be stretched to two thousand and more years to accommodate a supposed secret rapture; nor can this promise made to His apostles be arbitrarily re-assigned to all Christians living in a future generation.

He had prearranged to meet His apostles in Galilee (Mt. 28:7, 10, 16 & Mark 16:7), but because of their slowness to believe in His resurrection they remained in Jerusalem. It was there that He first appeared to them and received them as He breathed on them saying, *"Receive the Holy Spirit (John 20:19-25)."*

Additional appearances are recorded in John 20:26-29; Matthew 28:16-20; Mark 16:7-20; Luke 24:13-53; John 21:1-25 and I Corinthians 15:5-8.

The big mystery is why haven't we, who study the Scriptures and think ourselves knowledgeable in the field of prophecy, seen and accepted this explanation by Jesus

Himself before? Why haven't we accepted this obvious fact that this promise was made to His apostles and fulfilled in His post-resurrection appearances to them?

One reason is that, in our eagerness to glean every possible bit of information that we can about His return, as soon as we see the words, *"I will come again"* we are caught up in the assumption that it is a reference to the second coming and we quickly settle on that assumption without exploring the whole context for clarification and confirmation.

Further, we are all prone to be blinded and sidetracked by our own agendas and eschatologies which we always seek to support and defend.

We all ought now to be ashamed, humbled and chastised for ever thinking and teaching that John 14:1-3 was a rapture text, a funeral text or fulfilled by the coming of the Holy Spirit.

No doubt, pretribulationalists will either ignore this exegesis or they will fight tooth and nail to find some devious way to retain John 14:1-3 as a rapture text because without it they have no Scriptural support for their theory that Christ will return secretly and take Christians to heaven in the rapture.

Two things are certain in this John 14:1-3 text. One is that the promise was made to His apostles and must, therefore, be fulfilled in their lifetime. The second is that it was fulfilled *"in a little while"* after He spoke it.

There will be a rapture of the Christian church at His revelation, but nothing is said about that event in John 14:1-3.

UNIT THREE

CLARIFYING ESCHATOLOGICAL ISSUES

CHAPTER ELEVEN

WILL CHRISTIANS GO THROUGH THE TRIBULATION OR THE DAY OF WRATH?

Pretribulationalists make it difficult to answer this question because they wrongly equate the tribulation to the day of wrath. They fail to perceive that the tribulation and the day of wrath are two separate and distinct periods of time.

When they teach that Christians will not go through the tribulation they mean they will not go through that which is foretold in the Revelation chapters 8 through 19, but that is the day of wrath not the tribulation. According to Matthew 24:29, which briefly foretells the sixth seal signs of Revelation 6:12-17, those sixth seal signs occur after the tribulation of Israel. Those signs mark the beginning of the day of wrath (6:16-17) which continues through chapter 20 and concludes with the final judgment.

Thus, many mistakenly offer a simple singular reason for their belief in a pretribulational rapture. They cite what Paul wrote to the Thessalonian church—that Jesus, who will return from heaven *"...delivers us from the wrath to come"* (*I Thess. 1:10*) and *"God has not destined us for wrath, but for obtaining salvation through our Lord Jesus Christ"* (*I Thess. 5:9*). These verses speak about the believers deliverance from the wrath of God, but they say nothing about whether they will or will not go through the tribulation.

There are, then, two related but separate questions, "Will Christians go through the tribulation?" and "Will Christians go through the day of wrath?"

The answers to these questions are complicated by the fact, which many fail to take into account, that every time the word tribulation is used it is not necessarily referring to the same tribulation period or event; and every time the word wrath is used it is not necessarily referring to the same period or event. The context must dictate the use and meanings of these words.

Christians Presently in the Tribulation

As we fully explained in Chapter Three, the great tribulation of Israel predicted by Daniel 9:26-27 and Jesus in Matthew 24:15-28 occurred in AD 67-70 when Jerusalem was destroyed. The early church, including some of the apostles, lived through that tribulation. Jesus affirmed in Luke 21:24 that the effects of that tribulation will continue *"...until the times of the Gentiles be fulfilled."* Most agree that occurs when Jesus returns.

We also explained in Chapter Four that the great tribulation of the church began with the stoning of Stephen (Acts 8:1 & 11:19) and as forewarned by Jesus (Mt. 7:14; 24:9; John 16:33) and Paul (Acts 14:22; I Thess. 1:6; 2:14; 3:3 & Col. 1:24) it will continue to be experienced by the church until the Lord returns.

Christians on Earth During the Six Trumpets of Wrath

If, as seems probable, the Lord will return during the seventh trumpet period (Rev. 11:15; I Cor. 15:52; I Thess. 4:16) then the last generation of Christians will be on earth and have to endure the calamities that will then strike the earth as signaled by the sounding of six trumpets.

This is textually supported by the statement that the locusts (5th trumpet) will sting *"...only the men who do not have the seal of God on their foreheads" (Rev. 9:14)*. That not only implies that there will be men on earth with the seal of God on them, but it also indicates that they will be providentially spared the effects of this plague. While it is not specifically stated, I believe, the implication may be that the believers will be providentially protected during all of the trumpeted events.

Several Levels & Times of God-Sent Wrath

Every time the wrath of God is mentioned in the New Testament it does not necessarily refer to the time of the trumpets and the bowls. Different levels of God's wrath have been and will be manifested at different times.

In The Gospels:

The Coming Wrath = The Destruction of Jerusalem

There are only three references to God's *coming wrath* in the gospels—Matthew 3:7; Luke 3:7 and 21:23. All three anticipate the imminent destruction of Jerusalem and the great tribulation which will occur at that time.

In Matthew 3:7 and Luke 3:7 John the Baptist refused to baptize the Pharisees and the Sadducees and asked them, *"who warned you to flee from the wrath to come?"* The question presumes that they would be on earth when the wrath comes. That John was not speaking about the future trumpeted events or the bowls of wrath is evident by his affirmation that the wrath in question is near at hand. *"The axe is already laid at the root of the trees..."* and the unfruitful (unrepentant) ones will be *"thrown into the fire (the coming wrath)" (Mt. 3:10).*

Later Jesus would reveal the nature of the coming wrath; Jerusalem will be leveled and her people dispersed into the nations of the world. When the apostles would see Jerusalem surrounded by armies then her desolation would be at hand (Luke 21:20). There will be *"days of vengeance..."* and *"great distress (tribulation) upon the land, and wrath to this people" (Luke 21:22-23.*

Paul's letters to the Thessalonian church were probably the first New Testament books to be written—between AD 49-53, at least 18 years before the destruction of Jerusalem and the great tribulation of Israel. Therefore the wrath of which he spoke in I Thessalonians 1:10 may well have been the same wrath about which the Baptist had forewarned the Pharisees—the leveling of Jerusalem. While he commends them and characterizes them as waiting for God's Son from heaven he does not say that is when the wrath is coming or when believers will be delivered from that wrath. He only affirms that Jesus is the one who *"delivers us from the wrath to come"* without identifying the wrath or its timing.

In The Epistles:
The Coming Wrath=The Destiny of the Wicked

With the possible exception of I Thessalonians 1:10 as written above, when Paul writes of the coming wrath he generally is writing about the final destiny of the wicked to which they will be sentenced at the final judgment. When he wrote *"For God has not destined us for wrath, but for obtaining salvation through our Lord Jesus Christ..." (I Thess. 5:9)* he was affirming that our final state (our destiny) will not be wrath, but that doesn't rule out the possibility of encountering His wrath along the way.

This interpretation is born out in his letters to other churches in which he forewarned of the wrath to come. It is evident that in his letter to the Romans he refers to the final judgment and the eternal destiny of the wicked when he uses the terms *"the wrath of God."* *"For the wrath of God is revealed from heaven against all ungodliness and unrighteousness of men, who suppress the truth in unrighteousness"(Rom. 1:18).* In the remainder of the chapter he defines further the manifestation of the ungodliness and the unrighteousness of men and affirms that they are without excuse and that *"the judgment of God rightly falls on those who practice such things" (Rom 2:1-2).* They are *"storing up wrath for yourself in the day of wrath and revelation of the righteous judgment of God..."(Rom. 2:5).* Here he speaks of *"the day of wrath"* as *"the righteous judgment of God"* at which time he sentences those who do good to *"eternal life" (Rom. 2:7)* and those who do not obey the truth to *"wrath and indignation" (Rom. 2:8).*

Having established that he has in mind the final judgment and destiny of men when he uses the term *"the wrath of God"* in chapters one and two of Romans, it must probably be *assumed* it has the same meaning in Romans 5:9 when he writes, *"...having now been justified by His blood, we shall be saved from the wrath of God through Him"* and *"What if God...endured with much patience vessels of wrath prepared for destruction?" (Rom. 9:22).* Certainly that destruction takes place after the final judgment.

It is then also reasonable to expect the term to have the same meaning when Paul uses it in letters to other churches as in Ephesians 2:3; 5:6 and Colossians 3:6.

It seems, then, that the answer to the first part of our question, "Will Christians go through the tribulation?" is a definite, "Yes" since the tribulation of the church continues throughout this age until Christ returns.

The answer to the second part of our question, "Will Christians go through the day of wrath?" is also, "Yes" but with important qualifications, limitations and explanation.

When Paul writes, *"God has not destined us for wrath, but for obtaining salvation through our Lord Jesus Christ" (I Thess. 1:10),* he means that we'll not be sentenced to hell in the final judgment. We will get a more definitive answer to the question, "Will Christians go through the day of wrath?" as we study the coming wrath of God as presented in the Revelation.

In The Revelation:
The Coming Wrath=The Trumpets and the Bowls

The definable period known as the day of wrath begins with a world wide earthquake (Rev. 6:12) and the shaking of the powers of the heavens (Rev. 6:12-17; Mt. 24:29; Joel 2:30-31) as the tribulation period ends (Mt. 24:29). Since these are signs of the imminent return of Christ, Christians will still be alive on earth and the last generation will be present for the six trumpeted events until the Lord returns during the seventh trumpet period and transforms (I Cor. 15:51) and raptures them to Himself.

The Trumpets of Wrath

The presence of the people of God on earth for the trumpeted events is verified by the stated fact that the locusts that arrive upon the sounding of the fifth trumpet will hurt only those who do not have the seal of God on their foreheads, affirming that there will be present those who are sealed by God (Rev. 9:4).

The measurement of the temple and those who worship therein (the church) and the presence and ministry of the Lord's two witnesses may be further confirmation of the presence of the Body of Christ (Rev. 11:1-13).

The Bowls of Wrath

The summary statement in Revelation 11:18 of some of the events to occur during the seventh trumpet period includes *"...and Thy wrath came."* The day of wrath which began with the sixth seal signs (Rev. 6:12-17) and continued through the seven trumpeted events (Rev. 8:1-9:21) will be intensified after the Lord has returned (Rev. 19:15) in what is likened to a grape harvest (Rev. 14:17-20). Six bowls of wrath will be poured out with the seventh being the final judgment (Rev. 15:1-20:15).

Christians will also be present on earth during this day of wrath, but they will have been resurrected or raptured and be present in their glorified immortal, spiritual bodies, having been transformed and coming with Him in His Second Coming.

The following texts affirm our conclusion that the saints will be on earth during the trumpet and bowl series of events.

Present In The Flesh For The Trumpets

Revelation 8:3-4 The trumpet events will be sent in answer to the prayers of the saints.

Revelation 9:4 The saints are excluded from the locust stings.

Revelation 11:9 They are described as paying homage to God's two martyred witnesses.

Revelation 13:7 The beastly antichrist makes war with them.

Revelation 13:17 They refuse the mark of the beast.

Present in Glorified Bodies For the Bowls

Revelation 14:1 They are seen (represented by the 144,000) with Jesus on Mt. Zion.

Revelation 17:14 They are with Jesus when the beast and his allies war against Christ (at Armageddon 19:19).

Revelation 20:4 The resurrected martyrs and other saints reign with Christ for 1000 years.

Revelation 20:9 They are attacked by Satan in his last failing effort to overthrow Christ's kingdom.

Must we not then conclude that the answer is yes to both questions? Christians will be on earth for both the tribulation and the day of wrath.

However, the tribulation is not limited to a definable seven year period prior to or following the Lord's return, but is the prospective experience of the church throughout this present age.

CHAPTER TWELVE

VULTURES AND EAGLES

"Wherever the corpse is, there the vultures (eagles) will gather" (Mt. 24:28).

"Where the body is, there also will the vultures (eagles) be gathered" (Luke 17:37).

These cryptic proverbs spoken by Jesus, have puzzled students of the Bible as to their meaning and their application. Most would agree with the simple observation of D. A. Carson in the Expositor's Bible Commentary that "The proverb itself is a difficult one." I would add, therefore, it is easy to misinterpret Jesus' application of the proverb. It is probably true, as Sherman E. Johnson and George A. Buttrick have asserted in The Interpreter's Bible Commentary, that it is a secular Oriental proverb which Christ adapted for His own use and gave it a new application.

Proposed Meanings

Until my retirement from the pastorate I had not given these proverbs very much thought; and have, without great conviction or question, accepted the educated guesses that others had presented. An extended listing of proposed meanings can be found in William E. Biederwolf's The Second

Coming Bible. They range from the simplistic explanation by Moffat that the body is Christ and the vultures or eagles are His enemies, to the wordy and obtuse one by E. H. Plumptre in The Layman's Handy Commentary. He writes, "What the enigmatic proverb...means, is that whenever life is gone, wherever a church or nation is decaying and putrescent, there to the end of time will God's ministers of vengeance, the vultures that do their work of destruction, and so leave room for new forms of life by sweeping off that which was 'ready to vanish away'...will assuredly be found." That, in my studied opinion, is too general a definition. It attempts a perceived meaning of the original proverb, but not the specific application or use Jesus made of it.

This is also the weakness of many who, like Sherman E. Johnson and S. MacLean Gilmour wrote in The Interpreter's Bible that it means, "Wherever there is reason for judgment, the judgment will take place."

The Contexts

As I began to study these two texts in an effort to better understand their meanings and to come to an interpretation that I can teach with more conviction, I became aware of two important details which few, if any, take into account in their explanations of these proverbs.

#1. Two Different Proverbs

These two proverbs are not exactly alike. In Matthew 24:28 Jesus said, *"Wherever the corpse is...etc."* The Greek word is *p'toma,* which is properly translated *corpse* or *carcass.*

In Luke 17:37 Jesus said, *"Where the body is...etc."* Here the Greek word is *soma,* which is properly translated *body.* The significance of this difference will be shortly explained.

#2. Two Different Contexts

Jesus spoke two similar, but different proverbs because they were spoken in different settings.

The proverb recorded by Matthew was spoken by Jesus after He had predicted the soon coming destruction of Jerusalem which would be the occasion for the great tribulation of Israel.

The proverb recorded by Luke was spoken by Jesus while giving instructions to believers about their assembly for the rapture which will occur upon His return to earth. These things being true it must not be expected that the proverbs will have the same application or meaning.

Matthew 24:28

'Wherever the corpse is, there the vultures (eagles) will gather."

I am persuaded that those who believe that Judaism or the Jewish nation is the corpse in this proverb are on the right track. C. H. Spurgeon wrote, "Judaism had become a 'carcass,' dead and corrupt; fit prey for the vultures."

Others, with whom I agree, are more specific in naming Jerusalem as the corpse in Matthew 24:28. William E. Biederwolf in the afore mentioned The Second Coming Bible concludes that the proverb in Matthew 24:28 is "applied by nearly all writers to the destruction of Jerusalem." He cites Lightfoot, Owen, Wolf, Clericus, Wetstein and Hammond among those who believe that the carcass is Jerusalem.

I agree with the consensus stated above and with my preterist friend, John Bray, who writes in Matthew 24 Fulfilled, "The Jewish nation, and more specifically the city of Jerusalem, was the carcass..." However, I disagree with him and almost all others who wrongly identify the vultures or eagles as the Romans. The text and the context lead, I believe, to a different identification of the vultures (eagles). For *corpse* the Greek word is *ptoma*. It designates a downfall or that which has fallen; that is, the dead body or remains of something or someone that has fallen (dead). On this occasion the corpse, as most seem to agree, is Jerusalem, which city is going to be destroyed.

The Vultures

The Greek word is *aetoi*. Almost every scholar agrees that the word generally refers to *eagles* and probably should be so translated here. Some translators have substituted vultures for eagles on the false assumption that the proverb is intended to refer to a carrion eating bird, which they believe an eagle is not. Carrion is putrefying flesh, but neither the proverb or the context requires that we understand the corpse to be putrefied. Further, the Scriptures affirm that the eagle appropriately fits the proverb. Concerning the eagle, God said to Job, *"His young ones also suck up blood; and where the slain are, there he is."* Habakkuk wrote concerning the Chaldean horse men, *"They fly like an eagle swooping down to devour" (Hab. 1:8).* Therefore in this study we shall use the more correct translation—*eagles*.

The Context Provides the Meaning

Jesus' quotation of this proverb came at the very end of His answer (Mt. 24:4-28) to the apostles' question, *"When shall these things (the destruction of the temple) occur?"* Therefore, understandably and correctly, many believe that the corpse is Jerusalem when it fell. It is, however, wrongly believed by the many that the vultures or eagles were the Roman armies. The major flaw in that identification is that the proverb depicts the eagles gathering to a *corpse*, that is, a body that is already dead, not as a bird of prey that is coming to cause that death. The Roman armies came and were responsible for destroying Jerusalem and making it a corpse. In the proverb the eagles come after the death and destruction had occurred.

The Eagles are False Christ's and Prophets
Matthew 24:21-28

Matthew 24:21-28, at the conclusion of which this proverb is spoken, describes the confusion and tribulation which follows the destruction of Jerusalem. Jesus told His apostles not to believe the false prophets who would claim that He had come and could be found here or there. Some would produce great signs and wonders and attempt to mislead even the elect. The proverb explained the coming and the activity of these false Christ's and prophets who would take personal advantage of the situation. *"Where the corpse is (fallen Jerusalem), there the eagles (false Christs and prophets) will gather."*

As usual, a difficult text becomes understandable when we allow Scripture to interpret Scripture and when we allow the context to guide us to its truth.

Luke 17:37

"Where the body is, there also will the vultures (eagles) be gathered."

We dare not assume that this similar, but significantly different, proverb will have the same meaning as Matthew 24:28.

The Body—Soma

The word in Matthew 24:28 was *ptoma* which, without a doubt, refers to a dead body, a corpse. This word *soma* simply means a body without defining whether it is living or dead, the context determines that. About 12 times the word is used in the New Testament to refer to a dead body, a corpse. Most of the times (about 40) it is used to refer to a living body. I believe that the context will show that it is here referring to a living, not a dead, body.

In addition, it does not always refer to a physical or human body. It is often used to designate a group of people closely united in some fashion like a family, a social, ethical or organizational body. Thus, we speak of a body of believers etc. We are all familiar with the use of *soma* in reference to the church as a body, the body of Christ. *"So we...are one body in Christ" (Rom. 12:5)*. The church is *His body* according to Ephesians 1:22-23; 4:12; 5:30; Colossians 1:18, 24; of which He is the Head and Savior (Eph. 5:23; Col. 1:18, ; 2:19). See also I Corinthians 10:17, 12:27 and Ephesians 2:16, 4:4, 16 and Colossians 3:15.

The Greek word for vultures is *aetoi* which, as was explained in reference to Matthew 24:28, almost all scholars agree, generally should be translated eagles.

The Context Controls the Meaning

As we have previously noted these two similar proverbs were spoken in different contexts and the context of any word or idea must be a major factor in determining their meanings and applications.

In this Lukan text Jesus told His apostles that the time would come when they would long to see Him again. At that time some would try to persuade them that He had returned and could be found here or there. The Matthean text helps us to understand that the time referred to was the time of Jerusalem's destruction in AD 70. Both texts affirm that when *His day* comes it will be obvious and His coming and presence would be visible.

In Luke 17:24-36 He tells them how it will be in *His day* or *"the days of the Son of Man"* when He shall come and be present again. On the day of His revelation, which will occur like a thief, suddenly, while the world is going about its daily routines, the rapture will occur. Where two are in the field, at the mill, in the home etc. one will be taken and the other left. Those who are taken are the believers. Jesus' instructions to those being taken make no sense if they are sinners being taken away to their judgment and destruction. They are to be *taken* and *gathered*. They are not to delay this gathering by trying to return to their homes or attempt to gather any possessions. This means that they would have time and opportunity to do these things. This contradicts and refutes the common and unscriptural teaching that the rapture will occur as quick as the blink of an eye. Like Noah and Lot they will have the opportunity and responsibility to respond and participate in their rapture trip.

Where, Lord? Luke 17:37

The fact that Christians (the disciples if living at the time) would be the ones taken and gathered prompted the obvious question, *"Where, Lord?"* The proverb in question was His answer to that question.

Understand that the *eagles* are the ones to be taken and gathered; and they are taken to *the body* wherever it is. The only interpretation that makes sense is that the body refers to the body of Christ, the church. The body consists of *"those who have fallen asleep in Jesus"* and who will be brought with Him (I Thess 4:14). *"Those who are alive and remain until the coming of the Lord"* are the ones *taken* and *"caught up together with them (the body) to meet the Lord in the air"* (I Thess. 4:15, 16).

Pre-Trib Error

Some are forced to create a strange interpretation of this passage because they believe that the rapture occurs 7 years earlier, not at the revelation (Luke 17:30) of Jesus. They are forced to say that it is the wicked who are *taken* and *gathered* to be killed and the vultures will eat their bodies. I wish Dr. John F. Walvoord and others who believe this would tell us where it says that those who are taken will be killed; and why Jesus would bother to instruct unbelievers not to delay their departure for their supposed killing. The instructions seem to imply a willingness to cooperate and the option of obeying or not.

If the wicked are taken, then it will be the believers who are left behind to deal with the supposed trauma of the havoc, confusion and many deaths supposedly caused by the cars, planes, trains, ships etc. that are suddenly driverless and the chaos caused by the sudden disappearances of millions of people in industry and communities all across the world. This interpretation causes only confusion. Let us overturn this conclusion with the truth. *"Where the body (of Christ) is, there also will the eagles (those taken) be gathered"* in order to be raptured to meet the Lord in the air.

CHAPTER THIRTEEN

WHAT JESUS TAUGHT ABOUT THE FUTURE OF ISRAEL

I am not an expert on the nation of Israel and the continuing conflict between Israel and the Palestinians. What I am is a student of Biblical prophecy with a passionate and tireless desire to understand what the Scriptures and, especially, Jesus have to say about the state and future of Israel and the Jews.

I write with the scary and humbling knowledge that the study of the past, present and future plans of God for Israel is an extremely large and intricate subject. I need to continue to study this subject and to maintain an openness to further light from the Scriptures and from my brethren in the Lord who may have genuine expertise about this subject.

Two Extreme Viewpoints

My observation, right or wrong, is that many with a layman's interest in prophecy as well as many prophecy experts and teachers have only dabbled in the surface waters of the subject and have arrived at conclusions that are set in concrete so that they will not allow themselves to accept any changes in their present viewpoints.

There are two extreme, 360 degree opposite, viewpoints that are taught with respect to Israel's future.

#1. God Will Fully Restore Israel

Dispensational pretribulationalists and others teach this viewpoint as an important plank in their eschatological platform. They believe that Israel will rise to a dominant place among the nations of the world; they will be fully restored to the land between the Mediterranean Sea and the Euphrates River; they will rebuild the temple and resume the sacrificial system and services of the Old Testament law, and be totally restored and recognized as the chosen people of God.

They view the modern nation of Israel as the specific fulfillment of prophecy and a sure sign that Jesus is about to return. Further, they strongly emphasize the separation of Israel and the Church with each having a different purpose and inheritance.

In reaching these conclusions they major in Old Testament texts; using them, almost exclusive of any New Testament texts, to prove their theories. And they totally ignore what Jesus taught about Israel.

#2. God is Totally Done With Israel

Preterists and a substantial number of others teach this viewpoint. The foundation of this view is that Israel's place and purpose as the elect people of God was that she should serve as the vehicle by which God would bring forth the Messiah. Since the Messiah has come and accomplished His mission as the Savior of the world, Israel's place and purpose has been fulfilled.

In addition, since Israel had rejected their Messiah when He came, God destroyed Jerusalem and its temple and that ended the Jewish age, the old covenant and the maintenance of the nation of Israel as the special people of God.

Most who hold this viewpoint believe that the church has replaced Israel as the elect people of God under the new covenant.

Select Texts Support Both Views

I believe that adherents of both views are guilty of something that we all must guard against—building one's case for a particular viewpoint by selecting and clinging to those texts that seem to support it while neglecting and simply ignoring any other texts that would challenge and refute that viewpoint.

Some texts strongly forecast that because of her constant covenant breaking Israel will perish. God threatens in Deuteronomy 8:19-20, *"If...you forget the Lord your God you shall surely perish...like the nations that the Lord God makes to perish before you, so you shall perish."* See also Deuteronomy 4:26; 30:18 and Leviticus 26:38.

Other texts seem to contradict that and affirm that Israel will endure no matter what she does. In Leviticus 26:44 we read, *"Yet in spite of this, when they are in the land of their enemies (because of breaking covenant), I will not reject them, nor will I so abhor them as to destroy them , breaking My covenant with them for I am the Lord their God."*

One dare not simply decide to believe one text and reject the other, somehow they must be reconciled and both held to be true unless one foregoes any belief in the inerrancy of the Word.

I do not believe that these and similar texts are contradictory. It is only our inept perception of them and their contexts that does not allow us to see their correlation and harmony.

In seeking to properly understand the Biblical texts that relate to the future of Israel I do believe that the New Testament texts, especially the words of Jesus, must take priority over what the Old Testament has to say on the subject. It is the latest word from God on this and any other subjects. Hebrews 1:1-2 strongly implies that what has been revealed through Jesus His Son has priority over and possibly makes obsolete what He had revealed through the prophets. This is why I find it so incomprehensible and disturbing that no prophecy teacher or author that I have ever heard or read has ever referred to or given credence to what Jesus has taught about the future of Israel.

Israel's Place In History

We need to take a quick brief survey of Israel's past in order to understand her future.

Many prophecy teachers and commentators overstate the place of Israel in the program of God for the history of the world. One sometimes gets the impression that they believe the world was created for Israel and the rest of humanity simply get the crumbs that fall from her table. From the beginning of human history God's concern and the program of redemption always has been in the interest of the entire human race not just any one segment of it.

A Servant Nation

God had been historically involved with humanity for about 2000 years before the nation of Israel ever existed. God brought her into existence as a servant nation in fulfillment of His covenant with Abraham so that through her instrumentality the multitude of nations that would become the offspring of Abraham through faith might be redeemed. The reason for the establishment of the nation of Israel was summed up in *Exodus 19:5-6, "Now then, if you will indeed obey My voice and keep My covenant, then you will be My own possession among all the peoples; for all the earth is Mine; and you shall be to Me a kingdom of priests and a holy nation."*

Two things must be noted about this promise that Israel was to be God's *"own possession."* #1. This was a conditional promise—If...then! #2. God did not designate Israel as His exclusive possession. They are to be *"(His) own possession <u>among all the peoples</u>;* for *all* the *earth is Mine (My own possession)."* Israel was not to be His <u>only</u> possession.

All Her Covenants Conditional

Contrary to what is commonly taught, all of God's covenants with Israel were conditional (Deut. 28:1, 13). Most prophecy teachers confuse perpetuity and conditionality. Some covenants are perpetual and said to be everlasting, but that does not mean that they are not conditional. Participation in the perpetual covenants was always on condition of faithful obedience to God and His covenants.

The Old Testament records the obvious fact that Israel has repeatedly broken the covenant and suffered the threatened consequences. By and large Israel failed in her calling and purpose as the priestly nation that would lead all the nations into faithful obedience to her God. She became self-centered and proud of her supposed superiority to other nations and she expected the benefits of the covenants without meeting the conditions.

Rejection of Her Messiah

After repeated failures, captivities, dispersions, occupations by foreign powers and after God's many extensions and bestowals of grace, the straw that broke the proverbial camel's back was Israel's rejection of Messiah whom she herself gave birth to.

Consequence: Destruction of Jerusalem

As predicted by Daniel (Dan. 9:26-27) and Jesus (Mt. 24:4-28) Jerusalem and its temple were destroyed in AD 70.

AD 67-70 was a period of great tribulation for Israel (Mt. 24:21-28) which included the dispersion of her citizenry into all the nations of the world. She has continued to exist under that dispersion and tribulation to the present day. Even though the state of Israel came into existence in 1948 most Jews are still scattered among the nations and most of those scattered Jews, as well as those living in Israel today, are irreligious and living in unbelief and rejection of their Messiah.

Further, Jerusalem is still being *"tread under foot by Gentiles"* and Israel's people are not living securely or at peace in the land. All of which causes me to question those who believe and teach that the modern state of Israel is a fulfillment of Biblical prophecy. Was it an act of God or due mostly to the political success of the Zionist movement and its supporting nations?

Messiah's Judgment of Israel

It is a sad fact that today's prophecy teachers pay little or no attention to Jesus' teaching about Israel. By actual count I have at least 448 books on prophecy plus numerous commentaries and magazines that pertain to the whole range of prophetic themes including the future of Israel.

To the best of my recollection, not one—do not let the enormity of what I am writing escape you—NOT ONE (apart from a few preterists) of these authors, which include most of the well known prophecy teachers Hal Lindsey, Tim LaHaye, Jack VanImpe, Dave Breese, John Hagee, John Walvoord etc., etc. (give me a name, I probably have his book)—I repeat, NOT ONE gives any significant place in his eschatology to the teaching of Jesus when he expounds his theory on the future of Israel. They will quote profusely from the Old Testament and other writers, but no one seems interested in what Jesus had to say.

A summary of what Jesus had to say to and about Israel and her future follows.

Jesus' First Word To Israel: Repent

John the Baptist and then Jesus came to Israel as representatives of the coming kingdom of heaven and issued the same call to Israel, *"Repent, for the kingdom of heaven is at hand."* This initial persistent call for repentance was necessitated by her disobedience to and estrangement from God.

John and Jesus agreed on the severe penalty due to any Israelite and the nation if they did not repent. First, John told the Pharisees and Sadducees, who showed no evidences or fruit of repentance, that *"every tree therefore that does not bear good fruit is <u>cut down</u> and thrown into the fire (Mt. 3:10)."* Later, Jesus told the Jews, *"Unless you repent, you will <u>all</u> likewise <u>perish</u> (Luke 13:3)"* and then repeated the threat in verse 5. Were these idle threats? Certainly not! Many did repent and become disciples of John and then of Jesus. Many others, the majority, did not repent and must bear the consequences.

An Early Judgment of Israel Mt. 8:5-13

Coming into Capernaum after delivering the sermon on the mount, Jesus healed the son of a centurion to whom He said, *"Truly I say to you, I have <u>not found</u> such <u>great faith</u> with anyone in Israel (Mt. 8:10)."* With the acknowledgment that He had not found great faith in Israel He made a great bold judgment upon that nation. *"And I say to you (centurion), that many (like yourself) shall come from east and west (Gentiles), and recline (at tables) with Abraham, and Isaac, and Jacob, in the kingdom of heaven; BUT THE SONS OF THE KINGDOM (JEWS) SHALL BE <u>CAST OUT</u> INTO THE OUTER DARKNESS" (the place of unbelief) (Mt. 8:11-12).*

The outer darkness is described elsewhere as the place of those who are not chosen (Mt. 24:14), those who are without a wedding garment (righteousness, Mt. 22:13), those who are hypocritical (Mt. 24:51), those who are worthless servants (Mt. 25:30) and evil doers (Luke 13:27:28). There will be weeping and gnashing of teeth when they see Abraham, Isaac and Jacob in the kingdom of God while they are cast out (Luke 13:28).

Are we not to take Jesus' words seriously? Shall we dismiss them as just rhetoric without any historical reality? Is not He predicting that Israel will not maintain her place in the kingdom of heaven? He does not give up on this theme, He keeps returning to it and repeating it at various times.

Repeat #1. The Fig Tree Parable Luke 13:1-9
Some who heard Jesus teach made mention of certain Galileans whom Pilate had put to death and 18 people who were killed when the tower of Siloam fell. The implication was that they must have been great sinners for suffering that fate. In effect Jesus said that they were no worse than those who were talking to Him and all the men living Jerusalem. Sternly He warned them, *"Unless you repent, you will all likewise perish."*

Then He told this fig tree parable which was plainly meant to express how Israel stood before God at that time. It was an elaboration on the point just made that if Israel did not repent they would all perish.

"A certain man (God) had a fig tree (Israel) which had been planted in his vineyard (the world); and he came looking for fruit (of repentance) on it, and did not find any. And he said to the vineyard-keeper, 'Behold, for three years (of Christ's ministry) I have come looking for fruit on this fig tree without finding any. CUT IT DOWN! (get rid of it). Why does it even use up the ground?' And he said to him, 'Let it alone, sir, for this year too, until I dig around it and put in fertilizer; (an extension of grace for the remainder of Christ's ministry and the offering of the new covenant to them through the apostles after His death) and then if it bears fruit next year, fine, but IF NOT, CUT IT DOWN!'"

Repeat #2. Luke 13:22-30
In the latter days of His ministry as He journeyed toward Jerusalem He was asked, *"Are they few that are being saved?"* According to Jesus' answer, being saved was equivalent to entering the kingdom of heaven (Luke 13:27-30).

He answered those who asked the question by saying that many (Jews) will seek to enter and not be able to; and many will seek to enter after the door is shut. Then those Jews will say, *"We ate and drank in Your presence, and You taught in our streets,"* but Jesus will have to say, *"There will be weeping and gnashing of teeth when you see Abraham and Isaac and Jacob and all the prophets in the kingdom of God, but yourselves being cast out!" (Luke 13:28).*

Repeat #3. Luke 14:15-24
Shortly thereafter as He dined in the house of one of the rulers of the Pharisees one of the guests said, *"Blessed is he that shall eat bread in the kingdom of God."* Jesus responded with the parable of a great supper which, I believe, was again directed to the Jews who had made excuses and did not come to the supper. The master of the house sent his servants everywhere to bring in whomever they could find.

The significant *judgment* that pertained to Israel was spoken by the master of the house, *"FOR I SAY UNTO YOU, THAT NONE OF THOSE MEN THAT WERE BIDDEN SHALL TASTE OF MY SUPPER."*

Repeat #4. Matthew 22:1-14
The same point made in the previous parable is made in the parable of the king who made a wedding feast for his son. Those who were invited were unwilling to come and all ignored the invitation and attended to their own interests. *"But the king was enraged and sent his armies, and destroyed those murderers, and <u>set their city on fire</u>."* That precise judgment was fulfilled against Israel in AD 70.

In this parable Jesus added the important note that one must be properly attired with wedding clothes (the robe of righteousness) to attend this wedding. Those not so clothed (the Jews) will be cast out into the outer darkness.

Israel's Eviction Notice Matt. 21:33-45; Mk. 12:1-12; Luke 20:9-19

Jesus created quite a stir in the city of Jerusalem when He had entered it riding on a donkey. However, the next day when He cleansed the temple it was evident that opposition and animosity towards Him had intensified. *"The chief priests and the scribes and the leading men among the people were trying to destroy Him (Luke 19:47)."* They questioned His authority to do what He was doing. Then He boldly told them face to face, *"Truly I say to you that the tax-gatherers and harlots will get into the kingdom of God before you."* That set the stage for the parable of the vineyard or landowner in which He served notice that they were to be evicted from the kingdom of God.

Look first at the aftermath of the parable. The chief priests, Pharisees, scribes and elders understood that He was talking about them and their rejection of Him (Mt. 21:45; Mk. 12:12 & Luke 20:19).

When, in the parable, He revealed to them His knowledge of their intent to kill Him He asked the poignant question, *"What will the owner of the vineyard (God) do to those vinegrowers (who will have killed His Son, Jesus)?* Unknowingly they described their own fate when they surmised, *"He will bring those wretches to a wretched end, and will <u>rent out the vineyard</u> to other vine growers..."*

Jesus then pronounced this clear bold judgment upon the leaders of Israel..."*THEREFORE I SAY TO YOU, THE KINGDOM OF GOD WILL BE <u>TAKEN AWAY FROM YOU</u>, AND GIVEN TO A NATION PRODUCING THE FRUIT OF IT" (MT. 21:43).*

One will seldom, if ever, hear or read any of the leading popular prophecy teachers, preachers or authors even mentioning this prophecy. Why not? Because it does not fit in with the program they have decided upon for Israel.

If the kingdom was taken from Israel the next obvious question is, "To whom was it given?"

The Kingdom Given To The Church

Jesus said that the kingdom of God would be taken from Israel and given to a nation that would produce its fruit. I believe that nation was the Christian Church. I offer the following Scriptural support for that conclusion.

The Disciples to Receive the Kingdom Luke 12:32

After urging His disciples to seek the kingdom of God He told them not to be afraid because *"Your Father has chosen gladly to give you the kingdom" (Luke 12:32)*. The disciples were apostles-in-training who would become the foundation stones of the church (Eph. 2:20).

The Church Given the Keys Matthew 16:13-20

Later when He told Peter that He would build His church upon him and the other apostles (Mt. 16:18) He also said that He would give them the keys of the kingdom of heaven. Those who have the keys have access, entrance, control and possession of the kingdom. How much plainer could our Lord have made the fact that the kingdom was to be taken from Israel and given to the church?

The Word Nation (Ethnos)

Jesus' prediction was that the kingdom of God would be taken from Israel and given to a nation (ethnos) that would bring forth its fruits (Mt. 21:43). Do not trip over the word *nation*. The Greek word *ethnos* is used in reference to any multitude associated or living together, a company, troop or swarm. It does not have to refer to a political organization.

The Confirmation of Peter I Peter 2:4-12

It is certainly not coincidental that the very words used to describe the nature and purpose of Israel in Exodus 19:56 and Deuteronomy 7:6 were used by Peter to describe the nature and purpose of the church.

Even more significantly the word *nation (ethnos)* was used in reference to the church. It is a *"spiritual house, a chosen race (genos), a royal priesthood, a holy nation, a people for God's own possession and the people of God (vss. 5-10)."* This seems to be a deliberate effort to affirm that the nature and purpose of the church is the very same that was true of Israel.

In further support of this it is more than coincidence that when Jesus announced that the kingdom was to be taken from Israel (Mt. 21:42-43) He quoted Psalms 118:22. When Peter announced that the church is a holy nation etc. he quoted the same Psalm 118:22, *"The stone which the builders (the Jews) rejected has become the chief cornerstone (of the church)."*

The Kingdom Taken From Israel

In light of Jesus' predicted judgments of Israel to the effect that the kingdom would be taken from her; and Jerusalem and its temple would be destroyed, should we not look for and expect to find their fulfillment in the history of that nation?

Israel on Probation Luke 13:6-9 & Isaiah 5:1-7

The significant message of the parable of the fig tree, as written about earlier, was that Israel was not producing the fruits expected of her and, therefore, she should be *"cut down"* and discarded. However, the divine decision was to give her an extension of grace and to work with her in hope that she might still respond and produce her proper fruits. *"Until I dig around it and put in fertilizer; and if it bears fruit next year, fine; but if not, cut it down" (Luke 13:8-9).*

I believe that grace period included the remaining days of Jesus ministry to Israel and the years immediately following the crucifixion when Jesus worked with and through His apostles (Mk. 16:20) to offer the benefits of the new covenant to the Jews. It is carefully noted throughout the New Testament, especially in the Acts of the Apostles, that they and the Christian church witnessed, at the first, almost exclusively to the Jews. This was true in Jerusalem as well as all the communities into which the church was scattered when persecuted.

This was the case until it was obvious that the fig tree was not going to bear fruit; Israel continued to reject her Messiah and the gospel; and Israel was significantly responsible for the persecution of Christ's followers. Then the Christian witnesses, including Peter and Paul, turned to the Gentiles; and the Christian church, the nucleus of which consisted of a remnant of Jewish believers, eventually became a Gentile dominated church.

Israel Cut Down

After that probationary period of extended grace during which Israel remained fruitless, the threatened sentence must be implemented; Israel must be *"cut down."* And she was! In AD 67-70 the political center of the nation, Jerusalem, was destroyed along with her spiritual center, the temple.

According to the prediction of Jesus (Mt. 24:21) that was a time of great tribulation for Israel, and that tribulation would continue to plague her until her Messiah returns (Luke 21:24), the times of the Gentiles are fulfilled and the *"fullness of the Gentiles has come in (to Israel)" (Rom. 11:25).*

The olive tree (Rom. 11) was pruned of all the hardened unbelieving Jews. Only the remnant of believers remained and many wild branches from among the Gentiles were and are being grafted in.

Ever since AD 70 the hardened unbelieving Jews have been living in that *"outer darkness"* of unbelief and judgment where there is *"weeping and gnashing of teeth."*

Will Israel Be Restored?

I enter this phase of the study with fear and trepidation. Many believe in a full restoration of Israel. Before one can be 100% certain of a restoration for Israel a series of issues must first be dealt with; questions must be raised that have not yet been satisfactorily answered. #1. Does the new covenant wipe out any or all of the old covenant promises? #2. Does Israel's breaking of the covenant cancel out any of its proposed benefits and promises? #3. Have all the restoration promises of the Old Testament been already fulfilled in prior returns from Israel's captivities?

I do not have the answers to these questions and I do not believe the community of prophecy teachers have explored these questions sufficiently to give us firm and convincing conclusions.

These, then, are areas we continue to study while we share and explore the convictions we hold at this point in time.

Isaiah Chapters 10 & 11

There is no denying that the Old Testament frequently tells of a restoration of Israel. One, however, certainly must not conclude that every reference is about a future restoration. Most of such references (some believe all) were written before and during the Babylonian captivity and were fulfilled by the restoration that followed that captivity.

If we understand Isaiah chapters 10 & 11 correctly, Isaiah seems to acknowledge a first restoration and then prophesies a second one that is still in the future. Isaiah 10:20-34 seems to refer to the return of a remnant from Assyria. Then 11:1-5 speaks of the coming of the Messiah and the millennium which will follow (11:6-10). A predicted restoration seems to occur at that time. *"Then it will come about in that day that the nations will resort to the root of Jesse, who will stand as a signal for the peoples...then it will happen on that day that the LORD WILL AGAIN RECOVER THE SECOND TIME WITH HIS HAND THE REMNANT OF HIS PEOPLE...(ISAIAH 11:10-11)."*

If there is to be a future (second) restoration I believe the texts that express it make several important points about it.

#1. It will occur AFTER JESUS RETURNS not prior thereto.

#2. It will be a SELECTIVE REGATHERING of the REMNANT; only the true spiritual Israel as defined in Romans 2:28-29 and 9:6-7 will be involved, not all biological Israelites.

#3. They will SEEK THE LORD while still scattered among the nations first before returning to the land of Israel.

#4. Any restoration will occur within the context of THE CHURCH. They will become a part of the bride of Christ, the church, and whatever blessings they shall enjoy will be theirs as a part of the One Body that is in Christ, not as a separated part.

Did Jesus Foretell A Restoration For Israel?

Jesus, who foretold that Israel would be *cut down* and have the kingdom of God taken from her, did not, as far as I can find, make one clear statement that would affirm a future restoration of Israel. Nor did He say anything that would suggest that if she became a nation again that it would be a sign of His soon coming.

Subtle Hints: No Restoration

The harshness and finality of the judgments pronounced against Israel seem to suggest that in her present state of unbelief and rejection of her Messiah she may have reached a point of no return.

John the Baptist's strong word of warning to the Pharisees and Sadducees to the effect that *"every tree therefore that does not bear good fruit is <u>cut down</u> and <u>thrown into the fire</u>" (Mt. 3:10)* has a note of finality to it. Can a fig tree that has been cut down and burned be restored?

The same sense of finality is found in Jesus' words about the sons of the kingdom being cast out into outer darkness where there is weeping and gnashing of teeth (Mt. 8:11-12). Is recovery possible for those who are cast into *"outer darkness?"*

These statements by John and by Jesus seem to reflect a final state or destiny of the Jews. In Luke 13:1-9 He said that if *"all the men who live in Jerusalem"* did not repent they would *"perish."* Is not that a state from which there is no restoration? Later in the same chapter, verses 24-28, in answer to someone's question about how many will be saved, He said that after the door is shut, if the Jews are on the outside and knocking to gain entrance, they will be refused even if they claim, *"We ate and drank in Your presence, and You taught in our streets."* Then, He said that they will weep and gnash their teeth because their forefathers are in the kingdom but they are *"cast out."*

Jesus' statement to the apostles that in the regeneration they will sit on twelve thrones judging the twelve tribes of Israel (Mt. 19:28) suggests Israel's subjugation rather than their restoration.

Finally, He told a parable about the man who gave a big dinner and invited many (the Jews) who made excuses and did not come. He then invited others (Gentiles) and said,

"*None*" *of those men who were invited shall taste of my dinner.*" That seems to rule out a restoration.

Subtle Hints: Yes, A Restoration

On the other hand there are a few statements that may suggest the possibility of a future restoration of Israel. Jesus spoke of the time after His return as *"the regeneration."* If one understands this as relating primarily to Israel one might assume a restoration for that nation, but Acts 3:21 terms it a restoration of all things which would suggest a general restoration of the universe (Mt. 19:28). Further, as stated earlier, the following statement to the effect that the apostles will judge the twelve tribes of Israel may suggest subjugation rather than a place of prestige and power.

After weeping over Jerusalem and declaring that it would be left desolate, He said that Jerusalem would not see Him, *"Until you say, 'Blessed is He who comes in the name of the Lord'."* Some believe that this implies an acceptance of their Messiah when He returns. If that is so, that would require their individual repentance and subsequent regeneration, but not necessarily their restoration as a predominant nation. Christ, along with the church, will be the ones who will reign and dominate in the millennium (Mt. 23:39).

Luke 21:14 is the text that is most likely to suggest some kind of restoration, at least, of Jerusalem. Speaking of the imminent destruction of Jerusalem and the tribulation that would attend that event, He said that Jerusalem would be trodden under foot by the Gentiles *"UNTIL THE TIMES OF THE GENTILES BE FULFILLED."* That certainly implies that at that time Jerusalem would no longer be over-run or under the control of the Gentiles. But one may be reading too much into that statement to assume from it that Israel will be restored as a dominant nation.

The fact that we cite statements made by Jesus that both suggest and reject the possibility of a restoration for Israel does not mean that we believe Jesus contradicted Himself or did not know whether or not there would be a restoration of Israel. It only means that we do not fully understand these texts and cannot perfectly correlate them.

One Unified Body In Christ

I totally reject what is commonly taught by pretribulationalists who separate Israel from the church and place them on two separate tracks. I believe that their teachings on this matter are close to, if not blatant, heresy.

What Men Teach

The late Dave Breese and Dr. John Walvoord among others taught that the Jews will not be saved on the same basis as the rest of us; nor will they, when they are saved, become a part of the church.

The late Robert VanKampen (Pre-wrath) wrote that Israel must first atone for her sins. "Not until the natural line of Abraham has fully atoned for their iniquity, will God take off their spiritual blinders and ...bring in everlasting righteousness."

Hal Lindsey, who is alive and well on earth, wrote in his book <u>The Late Great Planet Earth</u> "For us, as believers, our hope is different from Israel's" and "There is a great distinction between God's purposes for the nation of Israel and... for the church."

What the Bible Teaches

<u>Jesus</u>

"I have other sheep (Gentiles) which are not of this fold (not Jews), I must bring them also, and they shall hear My voice; and they shall become ONE FLOCK (with) one Shepherd" (John 10:16).

Caiaphas

This high priest prophesied, *"that Jesus was going to die for the nation; and not for the nation only, but that He might also GATHER TOGETHER into ONE the children of God who are scattered abroad"* (John 11:51-52).

Paul

In Ephesians chapter two Paul wrote concerning the Gentiles, who had been *"excluded from the commonwealth of Israel,"* that *"now in Christ Jesus you who formerly were far off have been brought near (to the commonwealth of Israel) by the blood of Christ...who made BOTH groups into ONE, and broke down the barrier of the dividing wall...that in Himself He might make the two into ONE NEW MAN, thus establishing peace, and might reconcile them BOTH in ONE BODY to God through the cross..."(Eph. 2:13-16).* So then *"you (Gentiles) are fellow-citizens (of the commonwealth of Israel) with the saints (Jewish believers), and are of God's household..."(Eph. 2:19).* In Christ *"the whole building (Jews & Gentiles), being fitted TOGETHER is growing into a HOLY TEMPLE in the Lord,...being BUILT TOGETHER into a dwelling of God in the Spirit"* (Eph. 2:21-22).

How dare anyone separate what Christ brought together by His death? Later Paul wrote that we are to be diligent *"To preserve the unity of the Spirit in the bond of peace. There is ONE BODY...one Lord, one faith, one baptism, one God..."* (Eph. 4:3-6).

This unity is emphasized again at the conclusion of Galatians chapter three. *"There is neither Jew nor Greek,... you are ALL ONE IN Christ Jesus...Abraham's offspring, heirs according to promise"* (Gal. 3:28-29).

And in Romans chapter eleven Paul totally rejects the theory that Israel and the church are saved on a different basis with a different purpose and a different inheritance. Gentiles are grafted into the same olive tree into which *"if they (unbelieving Jews) do not continue in their unbelief, will be grafted in; for God is able to graft them in again"* (Rom. 11:23).

When the fullness of the Gentiles has come in (to Israel's olive tree) then *"all Israel (Jewish and Gentile believers) will be saved"* (Rom. 11:25-26).

No Distinctions Since Calvary

Since the shedding of Christ's blood as the atoning sacrifice once for all God makes no distinctions in His dealings with the Jews and the Gentiles.

<u>Romans 9:24</u> The elect are called *"not from among the Jews only, but also from among the Gentiles."*

<u>Romans 10:12-13</u> *"There is no distinction between Jew and Greek, for the same is Lord of all..."*

<u>Galatians 3:28</u> *"There is neither Jew nor Greek,...you are all one in Christ Jesus."*

No Advantage Being A Jew

<u>Romans 2:9-11</u> *"There will be tribulation...of the Jew first and also of the Greek, but glory and honor and peace...to the Jew first and also to the Greek. For there is NO PARTIALITY with God."*

<u>Romans 9:8</u> *"It is not the children of the flesh (biological Jews) who are children of God, but the children of the promise are regarded as descendents."*

<u>Galatians 6:15</u> *"For neither is circumcision (being a Jew) anything, nor uncircumcision (being a Gentile), but a new creation."*

Philippians 3:3 *"We are the (true) circumcision, who worship in the Spirit of God and glory in Christ Jesus and put no confidence in the flesh (being a Jew)."*

Israel and the Church

It is probably not quite correct or wise to say that the church has replaced Israel. According to Revelation 12:17 the church is the offspring of Israel (the woman). The church might be viewed as the second generation of Israel. The church is what the believing remnant of Israel has become. She is the present state or form of true spiritual Israel; the present state of the remnant—though hardly recognized as such because of the preponderance of Gentiles and the paucity of Jews in the church.

The church has the same calling and purpose that Israel had (Ex. 19:56; I Pet. 2:4-12). She will have the same inheritance and destiny—the new Jerusalem in the new heaven and earth.

The Present Nation of Israel

I am pleased and happy for the Jews that they have a homeland in which they may settle if they choose to do so, especially those who may be persecuted where they are. I pray that they may prosper and live in peace.

However, while repeating the disclaimer with which I began this study—I am not an expert on the nation of Israel and the continuing conflict between Israel and the Palestinians—I hold to and share the following convictions about the nation of Israel.

#1. I am not convinced that Israel became a nation as a fulfillment of any specific Biblical prophecies. Most citizens and leaders of the nation are still in unbelief; not only have they not first turned to God and accepted their Messiah, but most are not faithful practitioners of the Jewish faith. They are basically a secular pagan nation. This being the case, certain other convictions logically follow.

#2. Christians, while loving the Jews and the nation of Israel, must be discerning in their support of Israel. Not every national act and decision is necessarily a correct one or has the blessing of God on it.

#3. While loving, praying for and supporting Israel and the Jews, we dare not hate and not pray for and support the Arabs nor assume that they are always wrong in their actions.

#4. I do not believe that the emergence of Israel as a nation is a Biblically recognized sign of the end-times and the return of Jesus.

#5. I am convinced that simply being a biological Jew, an Israelite or an Israeli, does not give such a claim to the land of Palestine.

Many devout evangelical Christians share some or all of these stated convictions. Dr. John R. Rice, a well known hard-line fundamentalist who was certainly not anti-semitic wrote, "There is not a word in the Bible that indicates that every ungodly Jew has a right to take over any part of the land of Palestine that he wants because he is a Jew...I assure you that if you saw the plight of more than a million Arabs crowded out of their homes, their loved one murdered, their property taken, running for their lives, and now living on a bare subsistence in poverty in shacks and refugee camps, you would know that their hatred of the Jews is not the hatred of some natural instinct against the Jews, but the hatred that people have against criminals who have murdered and robbed. And let me say further that the present little group of Jews in Israel is not the fulfillment of prophecy...if communists do what the Jews did to Arabs, you would despise them for their sin. All right, then a good Christian ought to feel the same way when a Jew sins against others." (The article appeared in Escaton in 1977).

I have another clipping from an article titled <u>Biblical Significance of Israel</u> the author of which I do not know. "There are Christians and Jews who feel that modern Israel has no significance in Biblical prophecy today. They point to the same Scriptures to show that the Jewish nation will only be established when the Messiah comes or returns."

The author then makes this interesting point. "This position is held by some of the very strict Orthodox Jews in Israel. They do not recognize the modern state of Israel. They believe it has no legitimate right to exist because the Messiah has not established it.

These same Jews claim that the state was established by Zionist Jews for political purposes rather than by devout Jews for divine purposes."

Thus, while we continue to view some things as through a glass darkly, we continue to observe and know that when God acts decisively as He orchestrates the prophetic future we shall see His hand clearly and rejoice in His wise and sovereign ways.

CHAPTER FOURTEEN

THE DESTINY OF UNREPENTANT SINNERS: ETERNAL TORTURE OR ETERNAL DEATH?

A study of Hell as the destiny of unrepentant sinners is not just an academic exercise done in order to satisfy our curiosity or to deposit more information into our bank of knowledge. Those who reach that destiny may be our friends, neighbors or even family members whom we dearly love. May this pursuit of the truth as revealed by God motivate us to rejoice in our own salvation and stir up our compassionate concern for others around us that they may hear and respond to the gospel of the Lord Jesus who delivers us from our sins and saves us from that destiny.

When I first made a comprehensive study of all the texts pertaining to the subject of Hades and Hell I assumed that what I had come to believe about Hell as a conservative Christian would be reaffirmed and enlarged upon. However, I have learned from making comprehensive studies of other subjects that God often has a surprise or two as He expands my prior knowledge and sometimes compels me to change some things I had accepted without question and that had been commonly held to be true.

The Present State of the Unrepentant Dead

So far as we know, no one is yet in Hell *(gehenna)*. Upon death, the wicked go to the place that is called Sheol in the Old Testament and Hades in the New Testament. Sheol is variously translated and means *death, the grave* and *the nether world;* all of which indicate the place where the wicked are confined in death and await their eternal sentencing to the lake of fire (Hell) at the final judgment. Hades has basically the same meaning.

We are given only little snatches of information relative to the experience of the wicked dead in Hades. According to Jesus' tale about the rich man in Hades, they tremble in the fiery torment and agony of that place (Luke 16:14, 28; Job 26:5). The pit of Hades (sheol) is a hell-like place where the wicked begin to experience what they will more intensely experience in the lake of fire.

As Jesus experienced the agony of death He went into Hades to make a proclamation there (I Pet. 3:20) and seized the keys of death and Hades (Rev. 1:18).

According to the Revelation given to the apostle John, Death will continue to send many into Hades (Rev. 6:7-8) by means of war, famine, pestilence and wild beasts (evil kings) throughout this present age (Rev. 6:3-8).

Satan will be imprisoned therein for the 1000 years of Jesus' earthly reign (Rev. 20:1-7) until he is released and after his final battle with the Lord he will be cast into the lake of fire which is Hell.

During the final judgment, as God destroys the present heavens and earth (Rev. 20:11; 21:1; II Pet. 3:10-13), death and Hades will be emptied (Rev. 20:13) as all the wicked dead are resurrected to appear at the great white throne to be sentenced to experience the second death, that is eternal death in the lake of fire called Hell (Rev. 20:13-15).

The Final State of the Unrepentant Dead

The fact that Hell (gehenna) and the lake of fire are one and the same place and experience is affirmed by the fact that both are named as the place wherein the wicked will be finally destroyed (Mt. 10:28 & Rev. 20:14).

The Earthly Gehenna

South and southwest of Jerusalem was a valley named for the son of Hinnom, thus Gehenna. It had a notorious history as a place where pagan worshippers burned their children as an offering to their god Molech.

In anticipation of Israel's arrival and settlement in Canaan, God incorporated into their covenanted law a specific prohibition against participation in this ungodly practice (Lev. 20: 2-5). After Israel's arrival, the practice continued; due in part to their failure to obey God's instruction to drive out the pagan inhabitants of the land.

According to II Chronicles 28:3, in 741 BC King Ahaz compromised his faith and the holy covenant by participating in this evil worship as he sacrificed his sons to this fire. The context suggests that others before him had done the same; as did Manasseh after him (II Chron. 33:6). It had, evidently, become a common practice prior to the Babylonian captivity and Jeremiah had to vehemently condemn the practice (Jer. 7:31, 32 & 32:35).

It was with a broken heart that Jeremiah predicted that Gehenna would become a burial place where the dead bodies of Israel would become food for the birds of the sky and the beasts of the land (Jer. 7:32; 19:6-9).

By the time Jesus had come into the world, Gehenna had become a gigantic, stinking, ever-burning garbage dump where the bodies of criminals and the poor were disposed of.

It was the most unsavory and unappealing place on earth. It became, then, a metaphor for the final destiny of the incorrigibly wicked; and its name was borrowed to identify that place of eternal destruction that awaited the lost sinner.

The Eternal Gehenna (Hell)

Jesus spoke frequently of the eternal Gehenna and the Bible gives us much information and forewarnings about it. It is primarily a burning place; being identified as *"the furnace of fire" (Mt. 13:42, 50), "The hell of fire" (Mt. 18:8-9)* and *"The lake of fire" (Rev. 19:20; 20:10, 14; 21:8).*

So far as we know, no one has yet been cast into Hell. Presently all the righteous dead are in heaven and all the unrighteous dead are in Hades. The first two of whom we are told will be cast into the lake of fire will be the beast and his cohort, the false prophet, of Revelation chapter 13. The third person will be Satan, the devil. Presumably all his angels will join him (Mt. 25:41). Then at some point before the earth is destroyed so as to be made new, Jesus will judge and sentence to their eternal destinies all who will still be living at the end of the millennium (Mt. 25:31-46). At that time the unrighteous ones (goats) will be sent into the *"eternal fire which has been prepared for the devil and his angels" (Mt. 25:41)* as their *"eternal punishment" (Mt. 25:46).* Jesus spoke earlier of this judgment, which He called the harvest, when His angels will gather up the tares (goats) and cast them into the furnace of fire (Mt. 13:24-30 & 36-43).

Finally all the wicked dead will be resurrected, judged and cast into the lake of fire (Rev. 20:11-15). These will include those whose anger leads to the murder of a brother (Mt. 5:22), those who do not rid themselves of whatever causes them to stumble (Mt. 5:29-30), the hypocritical scribes and Pharisees and their ilk (Mt. 23:13-15, 33) and those who are *"cowardly and unbelieving and abominable and murderers and immoral persons and sorcerers and idolaters and all liars" (Rev. 21:8).*

The Nature and Purpose of Hell

What will be the experience of those who will be cast into the lake of fire called Hell? What will happen to them?

Three Major Views

Three major views are held by Bible believing Christians. It should be understood that those who may differ from us in their views about Hell are our brothers and sisters in the Lord who may love their Lord and deeply respect the Holy Scriptures as much as we profess to do. It is so easy for one to assume that any and all who do not believe as I do are not as dedicated and faithful and we quickly judge and condemn them for their alternate viewpoint.

#1. ETERNAL <u>TORTURE</u> (Eternal Punishment)

Many believe that in Hell God will punish sinners with conscious fiery torture forever. What happens to the beast and the false prophet will happen to everyone in Hell. They will be *"tortured day and night forever and ever" (Rev. 20:10).*

#2. ETERNAL <u>DEATH</u> (Annihilation)

Others believe that the Scripture reveal that after their long period of punishment in Hades and an unrevealed amount of time in Hell, the sinner will be destroyed as they are consumed by the lake of fire.

#3. ETERNAL <u>SALVATION</u> (Remedial View)

A far lesser number than those who hold to views 1 and 2 believe that God will purify and ultimately redeem all who experience the fires of Hell.

In my final pastorate in Kutztown, Pennsylvania, a fellow pastor stated his belief that Hell is remedial. The supposition is that Hell will purify or bring sinners to repentance and, thus, deliverance from Hell. It would seem that such who hold this view also believe in universal salvation.

I personally believe that this view is the weakest of the three. It is difficult to find any concrete statements in the Bible that would seem to support it and a whole lot that seriously contradict it. To prove this view one would have to first prove the doctrine of universal salvation, which I do not believe is possible.

That leaves us with two remaining views and the question embodied in the title of this chapter. Will sinners in Hell experience eternal *torture* or eternal *death?*

Examining The Issue

Some, who believe sinners will be tortured forever, like to defend their position by calling their interpretation the literalistic view. They, thereby, imply that those who believe in annihilation do not interpret the Scriptures literally. That is a gross falsehood. We shall attempt to show that those who believe in the eternal death or destruction of sinners are the more literalistic.

Similarities

Adherents of both views agree that Hell is a reality, a real place of some sort; that it is a fiery place and that the fire (whether literal or metaphoric) will burn forever. Further, in reality, they both agree that sinners will be punished forever; they differ as to the nature of the punishment.

Differences

As stated above the two groups differ in their understanding of the nature of the sinner's eternal punishment. The first group believes that sinners will be punished in Hell by being consciously *tortured* forever in its fires. There will be no relief or release from their fiery punishment. The annihilationalist also believes that sinners will be tortured in the fires of Hell, for an unrevealed duration of time, but not forever. They believe that the Scriptures literally and profusely teach that sinners will be burned up, destroyed and consumed by the fires of Hell which is termed *"the second death."* Their conscious existence will then come to an end.

My Personal Conviction

Now I am going to surprise some who know me personally, maybe even disappoint some of them and probably upset a few. I have been taught and accepted without question that sinners will experience unending excruciating eternal torture in the eternal fires of Hell. I have always believed and taught that.

However, when I decided to study this subject with an open mind and was eager to accumulate those texts that would clearly support my belief I ran into that proverbial brick wall. I found, to my surprise and disappointment, so little clear Scriptural support for the eternal torture of sinners. I was equally surprised and challenged by the overwhelming number of clear statements that affirmed the destruction and death of sinners in Hell. Sinners would be punished by eternal death not eternally tortured.

Since I was and am committed to taking God at His Word, I must believe what it clearly says.

Some Probing Questions

God is not displeased or vindictive with those who ask probing questions as long as their intent is not to doubt or disbelieve but, rather, are seriously in search of the truth.

Have you ever settled back and tried to imagine or comprehend the reality of being tortured by fire forever and ever; without break or end; every single moment of every single day; day and night for 365 days in a year; and the years become decades and the decades become centuries and the centuries become ages; and it just continues on—and on—and on—and on—and on relentlessly forever?

Have you ever thought about how we presently react to a little fire? One cannot stick his finger into a fire and hold it there indefinitely. If one accidentally touches a red hot stove he cannot leave it there. He touches it for just a split second. Instinctively, involuntarily he pulls it away. In the fires of Hell the whole being is aflame and there is no voluntary or involuntary pulling away from it.

It is proposed and believed that God will torture sinners in fire forever as punishment for 80 or less years of sinning; the number of years depends on how long one lives. If an unrepentant teenager dies he will be tortured forever for 13 to 19 years of sinning.

On the human level, even in our depraved state, that would be considered unfair, unjust. Criminologists would ask, "Is the punishment commensurate to the crime?" The principle that the punishment should fit the crime was established by God Himself; He built it into the covenantal law with the concept that one should give *"an eye for an eye, tooth for tooth etc." (Ex. 21:12-36 & Lev. 24:17-23)*.

It is a fitting question, then, to ask, "Does the eternal torture of sinners for a life time of sin fit the character of God as we have come to know Him through the revelations of Scripture and in our own redeemed lives?" I am not judging God, I am only asking questions. I hasten to add if God does decide and plan to punish sinners eternally for a lifetime of sin I must accept that and none of us can judge Him to be unrighteous in so doing. However, I do not believe that He so intends.

The whole matter boils down to one question, "What has God Himself said that He will do to sinners in Hell?" Let us be willing to lay aside our human arguments and assumptions and teachings of the past and read and accept what God Himself has said on this subject.

We shall present proof texts for both views and pray that the Holy Spirit will give us understanding of them and that we may be willing to cherish the truth they will reveal.

Texts Cited in Support of Eternal Torture

Try, as I did, I can find only two texts in the whole Bible that weakly support the view that sinners will experience eternal torture in Hell. I say that the support is weak because it is by implication or assumption. No statement can be found that says with clarity and certainty that all sinners will be tortured forever in the fires of Hell.

Matthew 25:41-46

In this familiar judgment of the sheep and the goats it is affirmed that the goats will *"depart...into the eternal fire" (Mt. 25:41)*. The fire is eternal, but Jesus did not say anything about how long the goats (sinners) would be there and what will happen to them.

In Matthew 25:46 Jesus repeats the destiny of the goats. They will *"...go away into eternal punishment!"* Jesus does not tell us what the punishment is; eternal torture or eternal death? Elsewhere He does tell us plainly that the punishment is eternal death.

Revelation 20:10

This verse is possibly the strongest support proponents of the eternal torture view can offer. It clearly affirms that the devil, the beastly king and the false prophet *"will be tortured day and night forever and ever."* There is, however, nothing in the text that says or suggests that this will happen to all who are sent into Hell. In light of many other texts, which clearly state otherwise, that idea must be rejected.

A third text Mark 9:43-48 is often mistakenly used to support the eternal torture viewpoint, but when understood it, in fact, teaches the very opposite. In this text Jesus speaks of Hell as the place..."*where their worm does not die, and the fire is not quenched.*" Many wrongly assume that the phrase means that sinners will always consciously exist, that the worm represents some core of their being that does not die. That is not true. *"Their worm"* is something apart from themselves which continues to live by feeding off their dead beings. This phrase is a quotation from Isaiah 66:24 which affirms that, while the worms continue to exist, the sinners, off of whom they feed, are dead corpses. The worm and the fire do not die, but the transgressors do.

It may be helpful to remember that the fires of Hell were prepared for the devil and his angels not for mankind. Secondly, that according to Jesus there will be degrees of suffering in Hell. Of certain cities He said it would be more tolerable for Sodom than for those cities in the judgment. That, at least, suggests the possibility of different lengths of time spent in Hell before ceasing to exist and perhaps different degrees of fire.

In summation, Scriptural support for the eternal torture of sinners comes from only two texts neither of which actually say that the torture of sinners will be eternal. Thus, the support is minimal and must be weighed against the numerous clear texts that clearly affirm the eternal death (annihilation) of the sinner. We shall now present those texts.

Texts That Support Eternal Death

If someone had asked me before I started this extensive study several years ago, "Pastor Bob, will sinners be tortured forever or will they be destroyed by the eternal fire?" I would have insisted, "Of course, they will be tortured forever. Annihilated? No way!"

Then, after failing to find any clear statements in the Scriptures to support eternal torture, I discovered about 20 texts which affirm that sinners will be destroyed in death. If

I want to be a good student and teacher of the Word, I must consider the possibility of annihilation.

I present those text without a lot of comment and urge the reader to read them with an open mind and to accept their simple and obvious meanings.

Psalm 37

The references to the righteous in this Psalm are about their eternal destinies, therefore, it is probable that so also are the references to the unrighteous. It declares that evil doers will be *"cut off"* and will be no more (vss. 9-10). The wicked will *"perish"* (vs. 20) and are *"cut off."*

Psalm 92:6-19

When God allows the wicked to sprout and flourish it is only *"...that they might be destroyed forevermore."*

Psalm 145:20

"The Lord keeps all who love Him, but all the wicked He will destroy."

Malachi 4:1-3

The wicked, which the prophet calls *"chaff,"* will be *set ablaze* and *burned up* so as to have not root or branch and will be *turned to ashes.*

New Testament Texts: Sinners Burned Up

The New Testament picks up on the Psalmist's revelations that the wicked will be *destroyed* and Malachi's declaration that they, like *chaff,* will be *burned up.*

Matthew 3:10-12 & Luke 3:17

John the Baptist likened the wicked to *chaff* and said that Jesus would *burn up* the chaff with unquenchable fire. Does that sound like eternal torture or eternal death and destruction? This is the first statement in the New Testament about the destiny of the wicked and it says they will be annihilated.

Matthew 13:30, 40, 47

Jesus affirmed what John said about the destiny of the chaff. In this parable of the tares and the wheat, Jesus said, *"In the time of the harvest (final judgment) I (Jesus) will say to the reapers, 'first gather up the tares (sons of the devil) and bind them in bundles to burn them up (Mt. 13:30)...in the furnace of fire' "* *(Mt. 13:42).* That sounds like eternal destruction not eternal torture.

New Testament Texts: Sinners Destroyed

One of the most important and often overlooked texts about Hell is—

Matthew 10:18 & Luke 12:5

Jesus told His disciples to fear God because He has the authority to cast one into Hell and there He is able to *destroy* both soul and body. The Greek word is *apolesai* which means what we generally mean by the word destroy—to put out of the way entirely, abolish, put an end to. Often it is simply translated *to kill.*

It is, then, not surprising and certainly significant that at least five additional texts consistently use the same word to affirm the fact that God will *destroy (aploesai)* sinners in Hell. They are Luke 13:3 and 5; John 3:16; Romans 9:22; Philippians 1:28 and 3:19 and II Peter 3:17.

Each of these texts say the same thing simply and clearly and they support the implication of Matthew 10:28 that God will destroy the unrighteous in Hell.

And to add to the profusion of proof texts for this view point, there are additional texts which say the same thing, but use other Greek words which also mean *to destroy.* Acts

3:23 affirms that they *"shall be utterly destroyed... ,"* that is, wiped out completely. II Thessalonians says that those who reject God *"will pay the penalty of eternal destruction away from the presence of the Lord"* and I Corinthians 3:17 threatens that *"If any man destroys the temple of God, God will destroy him... ."*

Three Most Convincing Texts

It seems to me that all the foregoing texts overwhelmingly compel us to believe the consistent message they bear—that God will annihilate sinners in the fires of Hell. Yet, the most convincing texts are yet to be presented.

Hebrews 10:27 and 39

If one goes on sinning willfully he faces *"a certain terrifying, expectation of judgment, and the fury of A FIRE WHICH WILL <u>CONSUME</u> THE ADVERSARIES."* How can God say it any clearer? Sinners will be consumed (burned up) by the fires of Hell not tortured forever.

Revelation 20:14-15 The Second Death

The final destiny of the wicked is the lake of fire, elsewhere named Hell (gehenna). What is the lake of fire? What do sinners experience there? It is THE SECOND DEATH! The lake of fire is the place wherein people die a second time; and they will remain dead and cease to exist for all eternity. There will be no resurrections, no reincarnations. All sin and sinners will be eliminated permanently from God's perfected world populated by perfect people bearing His perfect image.

The first death of the sinner is physical while the soul continues to exist in Hades. The second death is the death of the soul—the total being, body and spirit—in the fires of Hell. It will be just as Jesus said, *"God is able (and, I believe, will) to destroy both soul and body in Hell."* After his confinement and fiery punishment in Hades, the sinner will be resurrected for his sentencing and then cast into the lake of fire where, only God knows how long, he will experience continuing fiery torture until he is consumed and cease to consciously exist.

We could end our study at this point with the assurance that we have proven our case. The Bible profusely and consistently declares that sinners will be destroyed in Hell not forever tortured.

However, if there are still any stubborn lingering doubts, I have reserved the nail-it-down-clincher text for last. These final texts should leave no doubt that the sinner will cease to exist when he experiences the second death in the fires of Hell.

I Corinthians 15:50-54; I Tim. 6:16; II Tim. 1:10
These texts blended together prove that it is impossible for sinners to be tortured forever. They affirm that—

#1. SINNERS ARE AND SHALL REMAIN MORTAL NOT IMMORTAL
In order for sinners to endure conscious torture forever would mean that they must be, or become, immortal so as to never cease to exist.

#2. ONLY GOD IS IMMORTAL
The Bible clearly informs us that only God possesses immortality (I Tim. 1:17 & 6:16); only God consciously exists forever. Therefore we are all mortal. Man does not possess, as many teach, an immortal soul. As sinners we do not and cannot consciously exist forever and will not, therefore, be tortured forever.

#3. CHRISTIANS ARE GIFTED WITH IMMORTALITY

The logical question, then, is "How can Christians have eternal life and live forever if they are not immortal?" The good news of the gospel is that *"Our Savior Christ Jesus... abolished death, and brought life and immortality to light through the gospel" (II Tim. 1:10)*. By His grace God has offered and made it possible for redeemed mankind to become immortal.

Paul tells us exactly when it happens that a Christian believer will be gifted by God with immortality. It will occur when Jesus returns and the righteous dead are resurrected and the living believers are transformed in order to participate in the rapture and His return to earth (I Cor. 15:50-54). The dead will be raised imperishable (having been made immortal) and the living Christians will be *changed* as they *"put on the imperishable, and this mortal must put on immortality" (I Cor. 15:53)*.

However, the unsaved dead are not raised at this time and the living who are unsaved are not changed, they do not become immortal. They are destined for the second death and will cease to consciously exist.

A Summation

At least 13 separate texts clearly announce that sinners will be *destroyed* in Hell; some of them use strong qualifying words such as *altogether, utterly* and *forever*.

Four separate texts clearly announce that sinners will be *burned up* like chaff and tares. Two of those statements were made by Jesus Himself.

Jesus states the fact that God can (and the implication is that He will) *"destroy both soul and body in Hell."*

Hebrews 10:27 very clearly affirms that a fire will *consume* the sinner who continues in willful sin.

I Corinthians 15:50-54 reveals that the righteous will be made immortal so as to live forever, but there is no promise to the sinner that he will be made immortal so as to exist eternally and experience eternal torture.

Finally, Revelation 20:14-15 names Hell the second death not the continuing torture chamber.

What then should we believe? What choice do we have, but to believe the inerrant Word of God which repeatedly announces that sinners in Hell will be *burned up, destroyed, consumed* and engulfed in a fiery *second death.*

As Paul succinctly wrote, *"the wages of sin is death" (Rom. 6:23);* he did not say eternal torture!

To conclude on a positive note— *"He who overcomes...is not hurt by the second death" (Rev. 2:11)* and *"Blessed and holy is the one who has a part in the first resurrection; over these the second death has no power" (Rev. 20:6).*

And while we generally do not look forward to physical death and do all we can to delay it, God looks forward to it. He is happy when He can embrace His children and welcome them home. *"Precious in the sight of the Lord is the death of His saints" (Ps. 116:15).* For He intends *"...in the ages to come to show the surpassing riches of His grace in kindness toward us in Christ Jesus" (Eph. 2:7).* If you consider and appreciate the extent of God's love and grace with which He has blessed you during your sojourn here on earth, Ephesians 2:7 means, "You ain't seen nothin' yet." *"To die is gain" (Phil. 1:21)* and *"The day of death is better than the day of one's birth" (Eccl. 7:1).*

CHAPTER FIFTEEN

AN OPEN LETTER TO ANY AND ALL PRETRIBULATIONALISTS

Twelve years ago when I began to write and mail <u>Second Thoughts</u>, a Bible study periodical with a prophetic emphasis, the introductory article was titled, <u>Pastor Bob's Friendly Civil War With Pretribulationalism</u>. The first paragraph explained the point of view to be emphasized in the periodical and one of its purposes.

"This is one man's declaration of war. It is a war I wish was not necessary. It is a war of words. It is a battle for men's hearts and minds. It is a theological and doctrinal conflict. It is a war against deceit, false doctrine and human error. It is a declaration of war against *pretribulationalism*. This will be, as much as possible, a friendly war. It must be a friendly war because it is a civil war. It is a war within the ranks of the Christian faith. Yet, the battle is not against our brothers in the Lord, but against their false teachings and the arrogance of spirit that sometimes attends the proclamation and defense of their theories. The enemy is pretribulational*ism* not pretribulational*ists*."

After years of exposure to the several major schools of eschatological interpretations, and while continuing a lifetime dedication to personal study of Scriptural prophecy, I am totally convinced that pretribulationalism is a deceptive and contrived theory which distorts and confuses the simple, clear revelations of God concerning the Second Coming of Christ and related events. Pretribulationalism is not just an insignificant difference of opinion among Christians but is a humanly contrived system that does not flow naturally and obviously from the Scriptures. A newcomer to the faith and to the Scriptures would not generally arrive at a pretribulational understanding of the future were he to study the Bible in isolation. Someone must inform him of the gaps, the splits, the secret comings and goings that are supposedly taught by the Word, because they are not stated anywhere in the Bible.

Hopefully, this chapter will help to explain why, throughout this book, we have periodically specifically pointed out what we perceived to be errors and weaknesses of that persuasion.

To state further the reasons why I stand opposed to that system, and in hope that some pretribulationalists may be open minded enough and challenged to take an honest reappraisal of their beliefs, I conclude with this open letter to any and all pretribulationalists.

Dear Christian Brothers and Sisters,

I rejoice with you in our common salvation as we bask together in the grace of God whereby we have been washed clean of all sin in the shed blood of our Lord Jesus and caused to be born again by God through His Spirit and His Word.

I share with you a high regard for the Scriptures, believing them to be inerrant and meant to be interpreted literally except where literary devices such as symbolism, allegory, metaphors, parables etc. are obviously used.

I wish to share four major reasons why I cannot accept your pretribulational theories and by which I hope to challenge each of you to step back and take an honest reevaluation of what you have been taught and believe.

Pretribulationalism Has Weak & Unscriptural Foundations

I grew up in a Christian environment wherein whatever eschatological teaching and preaching I heard was mostly of the dispensational pre-trib variety. While I did not totally reject it nor did I totally embrace it.

Concerning Daniel 9:26-27 I was told: #1. That a *gap* exists between the 69th and 70th week. #2. That the 70th week will be a *future seven year tribulation period.* #3. That the coming prince is *the antichrist* who will make *a covenant* with Israel. #4. That the *abominations* which effect the *destruction of the city* and sanctuary are yet to come.

Concerning the Second Coming and the rapture I was told: #1. That the *Second Coming* is *split* into two trips seven years apart. #2. That the first trip and the rapture will be *secretive* and *sudden* as the blink of an eye. #3. That the *rapture* occurs seven years *before the revelation* of Jesus. #4. That the raptured ones will be *taken to heaven.* #5. That the restrainer of II Thessalonians 2:6 is the Holy Spirit. And, of course, #6. the rapture precedes the tribulation.

These are eleven of the premises upon which the elaborate pretribulational eschatology is built, but I could not find *any* of these major tenets that I was being taught simply and literally stated in the Bible. Do not overlook the enormity of this fact. **NOT ONE VERSE CAN BE FOUND IN THE WHOLE BIBLE THAT CLEARLY STATES AND AFFIRMS THAT ANY ONE OF THESE ELEVEN PREMISES IS TRUE!** My friends, should not that fact scare you a little bit and, at least, cause you enough concern to make an honest reappraisal of what you have been taught and believe.

All of the above premises are arrived at by deductive reasoning, assumptions and arbitrary assignment of desired meanings. Since the whole foundation of pretribulationalism lacks clear Biblical statements to support what it believes, it is building its house on sand and is sure to eventually collapse.

Pretribulationalism Is Not As Literalistic As It Boasts

One cannot read much pretribulational literature without reading soon and often their proud boast that they are literalists when interpreting the eschatological texts of the Bible. Over and over and over again, ad nauseam, they clamor, "We are the literalists." The implication and the assumption intended by the use of the definite article is that only they read and interpret the Bible literally. All who differ from their interpretations hold erroneous beliefs because they fail to accept the Bible literally. And lest you miss that implication they will tell you again and again, "If you take the Bible literally you will inevitably come to pretribulationalism." I beg to differ with that presumption. It was when I read and accepted the eschatological texts literally that I came to a modified historical posttribulational interpretation and the weaknesses and errors of pretribulationalism became apparent.

One of the pre-trib authors who leans heavily on the boast of literalism to support his interpretation of the end times is Dr. Tim LaHaye. Sometime ago when I read his book <u>No Fear of the Storm</u> I got the strong impression that because there was so little Scriptural support for his viewpoint he had to repeatedly re-enforce his argument by telling us that pre-tribbers were literalists and, therefore, they had to be right. It is the theory of modern advertising that if you repeat something often enough people may believe it and buy your product. This boast of literalism helps to divert attention away from an otherwise weak argument by creating a public image of pre-tribbers as the *good guys* in the white hats and all dissenters as the *bad guys* in the black hats.

It is understandable for pre-tribbers to repeatedly tell us that they are literalists because it is not at all obvious in their presentations of their beliefs. Having read about a hundred or more of your books and having listened to many of your oral teachings, it is my perception that, while you pay lip service to the principle of literalism, when interpreting some of the key prophetic texts, in spite of your boasts, you frequently reject the literal meaning of those texts and supplant it with your own. This is especially true as you interpret Jesus' Olivet Discourse.

Matthew Chapter 24

Why don't you take Jesus' words literally and believe Him when He said about false Christs, wars and rumors of wars, famines and earthquakes, *"that is not yet the end" (Mt. 24:6),* but rather *"...the beginning of birth pangs" (Mt. 24:8).* I keep hearing your sermons declaring these things as proof-signs that Jesus' coming is imminent and, yet, Jesus was saying that these things were not even to be considered signs of the birth of the temple's destruction.

Why don't you take Jesus' words literally and believe Him when He said to the apostles that *you (meaning they)* will hear and see those things listed in Matthew 24:4-7 for this shall occur before the apostolic tribulation (Mt. 24:9) and, therefore, the end they were anticipating and the event that was to be born would occur in their lifetime?

Why don't you take Jesus' words literally and believe Him when He said that those things listed in Matthew 24:10-14 would occur *"at that time" (Mt. 24:10)* when the apostles will face tribulation and martyrdom (Mt. 24:9)?

Why don't you take Jesus' words literally and believe Him when He said that *you* (apostles) would see *"the abomi-*

nation of desolation which was spoken through Daniel"(Mt. 24:15) and *"Jerusalem surrounded by armies" (Luke 21:20)?* Therefore, its fulfillment must have been in their lifetime, which it was in the AD 70 destruction of Jerusalem and its temple.

Why don't you take Jesus' words literally and believe Him when He told the apostles that when they would see the signs foreshadowing the temple's destruction as mentioned above that *"then there will be (and there was) a great tribulation"* of Israel (Mt. 24:21 & Luke 21:22-25). He did not say that it would happen more than two thousand years later.

Why don't you take Jesus' words literally and believe Him when He said that the great tribulation which occurred in AD 67-70 was *"...such as has not been since the beginning of the world until now, nor ever shall (be again)" (Mt. 24:21).* A future great tribulation of that magnitude for Israel is ruled out. There is no prediction anywhere of a future seven year great tribulation.

Why don't you take Jesus' words literally and believe Him when He Himself stated the point of the fig tree parable, *"...even so you too, when you (apostles) see all these things (Mt. 24:4-28), recognize that he (or it—the destruction of the temple) is near, right at the door?"* He never said anything about Israel or their becoming a nation in this fig tree illustration.

Why don't you take Jesus' words literally and believe Him when He spoke of His *coming* and used the word parousia *which means when He arrives and continues to be present—"Then there shall be two men in the field; one will be taken (in the rapture), and one will be left..." (Mt. 24:40).* He never said anything about a rapture taking place seven years before His parousia.

I know this is getting repetitious and possibly monotonous, but I must continue to show how much those who boast of being literalists really are not such.

Peter and Paul

Why don't you take Peter's words literally and believe him when he instructed the church to *"fix you hope completely on the grace to be brought to you at the revelation (public visible unveiling) of Jesus Christ" (I Pet. 1:13)* — not at a supposed secret rapture and private coming seven years earlier.

Why don't you take Paul's words literally and believe him when he wrote that Christians will be *"...alive, and remain until the coming (parousia — arrival and presence) of the Lord"* and that they will be *"caught up"* (raptured) at that time (I Thess. 4:17).

Why don't you take Paul's words literally and believe him when he wrote that *"the day of the Lord,"* which includes *"The coming (parousia) of our Lord Jesus Christ and our gathering together to Him"* follows the apostasy and the revelation of the lawless one (II Thess. 2:1-2).

The same question could be raised about other passages as well. Why don't you take Daniel 9:24-27 literally where God said that 490 years would pass until Messiah would come and accomplish the atonement as promised in Daniel 9:24 rather than adding an indeterminable number of years to it.

Why don't you take Jesus' words literally and believe Him when He said in Luke 17:30-36 that the rapture of Christians will take place at His revelation, that is His visible public appearance, and not seven years earlier.

Dr. Tim LaHaye is honest enough to say on page 69 of his book, No Fear of the Storm, "one objection to the pre-tribulation Rapture is that no one passage of Scripture teaches the two aspects of His Second Coming separated by the tribulation. This is true" (underlining mine). That is exactly why pretribulationalism should be rejected. Many are rejecting it. Ever since about the 1950s there has been a notable shift away from pretribulationalism. The departure is reaching significant proportions. Dr. LaHaye's book, itself, was a testimony to the growing number of losses. In his introduction he acknowledges that he was motivated to write the book because five prominent friends had turned away from their long held belief in pretribulationism.

It is my hope and prayer that you, my beloved brothers and sisters in the Lord who are in the pre-trib camp, will begin to consistently read the Word and take it literally and join the ranks of those who are departing the deception of pretribulationalism.

Pretribulationalism Is Confused, Deceived And Sadly Wrong About the Great Tribulation

Your failure to accept the Word literally and your tendency to introduce theories that are not specifically and clearly stated in the Scriptures has led you to produce the concept of a seven year great tribulation that is wrought with gross error. Contrary to what you believe and teach, the Bible nowhere predicts a seven year tribulation period. The Bible nowhere says that the tribulation period follows the rapture. The Bible nowhere states that the great tribulation of Matthew 24 will be world wide. The Bible nowhere says that Christians will miss the great tribulation and added to these errors you wrongly believe that the great tribulation and the day of wrath cover the same time period.

As we taught in Chapter Three of this book, the great tribulation predicted by Jesus in Matthew chapter 24 was a local Jewish tribulation which came to pass in AD 67-70 and is not to be repeated anytime in the future (Mt. 24:21).

The great tribulation cited in Revelation 7:14 is a reference to the tribulation of the church which began with the stoning of Stephen (Acts 8:1; 11:19) and will continue throughout this age until Christ returns.

Since there are no other references to a great tribulation in the Bible there is no Scriptural support for a future seven year great tribulation. Since the only great tribulations depicted in Scripture have already begun and will continue throughout this age until the Lord returns—the rapture must obviously be posttribulational and will occur at the revelation (visible public appearance) of Christ.

It also follows, then, that Revelation chapters 8-19 do not depict the great tribulation, but rather the day of wrath.

Pretribulationalism Has An Imposed and Biased Interpretation of the Revelation

To those of us who are outside the pretrib fold it is apparent that you arbitrarily assign meanings to some of the ingredients of the Revelation that the context does not support. You impose your elaborately constructed system on the book instead of allowing the book to tell its own story. I offer the following examples of what I believe are arbitrary and unwarranted treatments of the text.

Revelation 1:19 The Content of Revelation

You are bound to develop an erroneous interpretation of the Revelation when you woodenly accept the nineteenth verse of chapter one as a chronological index of the book's subject matter instead of a general statement of what John is asked to write.

"Things you have seen" does not apply only to the vision of Christ in chapter one as you teach. That vision continues through chapters two and three which you say is limited to *"the things that are."* In addition, John will be shown other things about which he is then to write.

"The things that are" certainly includes the affairs of the seven churches in chapters two and three, but is not limited thereto. You are inconsistent in the use of your own outline. You tell us that chapters two and three contain *"the things that are"* and pertain to the time the Revelation was written, but then you teach that the seven churches represent seven

periods of church history. That, then, makes them a revelation of *"things which shall take place after these things."*

This leads to two more inconsistencies. First, it allows you to teach the error that *"the hour of testing"* in Revelation 3:10 is a reference to a latter day great tribulation rather than a happening during the history of the Philadelphian church.

Second, while teaching that the seven churches represent seven successive periods of church history you also teach that the rapture and the return of Christ always have been imminent. How could that possibly be true if, according to your own teaching, the Lord will come during the Laodicean period?

You correctly observe that *"things which shall take place after these things"* pertains to events in chapters 4-22, but you fail to perceive that not every event in those chapters are prophetic with a future fulfillment. Chapters four, five and twelve are not prophecies but historical flashbacks to the time of Christ's death and ascension. Viewing them as prophecies with a future fulfillment further distorts your understanding of the Revelation.

Revelation 4:1-2 The Rapture?

Your credibility as exegetes and teachers of the Word hits its lowest point, and the weakness of your position is most evident, when you arbitrarily introduce the rapture into the Revelation at 4:1-2.

These verses are all about, and only about, the time and circumstances when John was granted an *"in the Spirit"* visit into heaven. It says nothing, nor is it intended to convey anything, about the rapture. This is one of several instances where you impose your eschatological system on the Revelation in order to make it say what you want it to say.

Revelation 6:1-2 The White Horse Rider

Once again you force your system on the text when you arbitrarily identify the white horse rider as the antichrist. What textual support can you give for that identification? None! The antichrist or the beast has not yet been introduced in the Revelation. If one were reading the Revelation for the first time he would not even know there was an antichrist or a beast. There is nothing to this point in the book that would cause one to consider him as the rider of the white horse. The beast is not introduced into the tale until Revelation 11:7.

The details given in the Revelation thus far and the flow of the text compel us to identify the white horse rider as the blood bought church going forth in obedience to the great commission. The textual support for this identification is ample.

#1. The Earlier Context: Seven admonitions to overcome in chapters two and three.

One is meant to be impressed by the fact that seven times in His letters to the seven churches (representing the universal church) Jesus and the Spirit urge the churches to *overcome*. The Greek word is *nikao* which is elsewhere, including in 6:2, translated *conquer*. So in the breaking of the seven seals the tribulated history of the church unfolds as the church goes forth *"conquering and to conquer"* or *"overcoming and to overcome."*

#2. The Immediate Context: A celebration of the church as a kingdom of priests in 5:9-10.

John was given a flashback vision of Jesus' return into heaven at which time there was a celebration of His purchase of the church as a *"kingdom and priests to our God"* with the promise that they would *"reign upon the earth."* If they are a kingdom and expected to reign they must go forth conquering and to conquer. So they were given a *crown* (6:2) representing their kingdom status and they had a bow with which to do battle.

#3. The Identifying Color: White

The color of the horses were intentionally assigned to them by God to identify the nature of the riders. In the Revelation the color white is always used to identify something pure or someone who is righteous and good—never someone or something evil. It is totally inappropriate as a symbol of the antichrist and is not so used here.

To this point in the Revelation (6:1-2) we have already been introduced to Jesus' hair which was white as wool (1:4), a white stone (2:17) and white clothing (3:4-5; 3:18 and 4:4).

#4. The Identifying Fifth Seal: Revelation 6:9-11.

The fifth of each series identifies the group that is the target or subject of that series. We shall discover that the fifth bowl was poured out on *"the throne of the beast; and his kingdom became darkened" (6:10)*. The fifth trumpet called for a plague of locusts which were permitted to hurt *"only the men who do not have the seal of God" (9:4)*. And now the fifth seal revealed *"the souls of those who had been slain because of the word of God, and because of the testimony which they had maintained" (6:9-11)*. These are the Christian martyrs who were among those who went forth *"conquering and to conquer."*

While there are these several textual reasons for identifying the white horse rider as the church, there is no textual warrant to identify the rider as the antichrist. This erroneous identification of the white horse rider by pretribulationalists as the antichrist distorts much of their interpretation that follows in the Revelation.

Revelation 7:1-17 The 144,000

You make two huge errors regarding the 144,000. You tell us that they are *future fruits* of the gospel, that is, believers in the end times; but Jesus calls them the *first fruits* (Rev. 14:4) which identifies them as the early Jewish church. That is confirmed by James 1:18 as James wrote to *"the twelve tribes who are dispersed."*

There is general agreement, even among pretribulationalists, that twelve and its multiples is symbolic of the church. Thus, the perfected church, the new Jerusalem, has 12 gates, 12 angels, the names of 12 tribes on its gates, the names of the 12 apostles on the 12 foundation stones. The city is 12,000 stadia high, wide and long with a wall 6 times 12 (72) yards high. Thus the 144,000 represent the total church in its infancy when it was totally Jewish.

Then you arbitrarily say that they are evangelists, but neither I nor you can find that affirmed in the Bible.

Because of your erroneous belief in a future seven year tribulation you tell us the great multitude in Revelation 7:9 which no one can number all come out of those supposed seven years between the rapture and revelation of Jesus. The great multitude is what the 144,000 will have grown into; they are the full fruits or the final fruits who have come out of the great tribulation of the church which began with the stoning of Stephen (Acts 8:1 & 11:19) and will conclude at the coming of Jesus.

Revelation 19:11 Jesus on a white Horse

Your insistence that Revelation 19:11 depicts the return of Christ on a white horse is unsupportable by any other text that speaks of that event. In the first place the text does not say John saw Jesus *coming* to earth on a white horse. There is not a confirming word anywhere in the Bible that says that there are any horses in heaven or that Jesus and His armies will return on white horses. The angel, who at His ascension foretold His return, said that it would be just the same as when they saw Him depart—and they did not see Him depart on a white horse.

What John saw was a vision of how Jesus will appear when here on earth fighting His battles for control of the world. He is symbolically presented as a victorious and righteous warrior as He will smite the nations, rule them with a rod of iron and tread the winepress of the fierce wrath of God (Rev. 19:15).

This vision (19:11) was like those in Revelation 12:1 and 3 and 15:1. The signs and the visions appeared in heaven but the actions depicted by the visions took place on earth.

When the nations gather at Armageddon (16:16) it will be for the specific purpose of warring against Him who sat on the white horse (19:19). Therefore, He must already be on the earth and seen by the beast and the allied kings else one would have to believe that they assembled to war against Christ while He was still in heaven.

Growth Involves Change

In our study of and obedience to the Scriptures we ought to believe some basic core doctrines which we can and will defend; and because they are so clearly taught in the Bible we will allow no one to dissuade us from them.

And our faith should have sufficient stability so that we do not easily and quickly change from one doctrinal position to another. We do not profit by developing itching ears that are ever ready to be tickled by every novel interpretation that the imagination of man can provide and would-be theologians dream up.

On the other hand, if we are to grow in our knowledge of the Word and in our faith, we must be open to credible and Scripturally supportable revelations and interpretations that may differ from what we have here-to-fore believed and possibly have never examined or investigated carefully.

When we think we are standing fast and defending the faith as we stubbornly cling to what we have always believed, in reality, we may simply be stagnating in the doctrinal rut others have said we must follow.

We ought not be afraid to change even long held favorite beliefs if and when, as we mature in the faith and our understanding of the Word, it is clearly shown that the Word supports an interpretation that is different from what we have been taught and assumed to be true for many years. Growth involves change, usually in slow almost unnoticeable increments, but other times, especially in spiritual growth, it may occur in spurts and giant steps as the Spirit opens our eyes and gifts us with an ever expanding knowledge of our God and His Word.

Conclusion

My dear brothers, I do not expect that you will all be convinced of the error of your position and suddenly drop an interpretation you have loved and held for a long time. I do hope that some of you will have been seriously challenged to consider some of these objections to your theories and you will honestly take a second look at what you believe. I hope also that you will understand that those who differ from you are equally sincere in pursuing the truth of God's Word while believing in its inerrancy and intending to accept it literally.

Have a good eternity,
Robert L. Kramer

As we all travel rather swiftly into the future that God is planning for us and we anticipate the critical jointure of our Lord's return, we cannot say that we are there yet, but we are getting closer.

As we anticipate our future and the enjoyment of it in our perfected state, we see Him and our future..."*with unveiled face beholding (Him and it) as in a mirror.*" But we are *"being transformed into His image from glory to glory,"* that is also in small increments. May it be true also of our perfection that while we cannot say we are there yet we are getting closer.

ADDENDUM

THE PURPOSE OF PROPHECY

Prophecy is a major component of the Bible. It is a thread that runs through the whole book and holds it all together. It is not an incidental by-product or fringe accompaniment to the message of the Holy Scriptures. It is the heart and soul of it. Therefore the study of prophecy must not be one's spiritual hobby to indulge in at leisure. It is not a plaything to fill the idle hours of ones spiritual journey. One must not dabble in prophecy. It is too important and such an integral part of the whole of the Scriptures to be handled piecemeal or haphazardly. I would propose that the Scriptures ascribe at least four purposes for the pursuit and study of prophecy.

The Primary Purpose: To Glorify God

Prophecy is not intended to satisfy our idle curiosity nor to enhance our personal reputations as being expert or knowledgeable above others. Nor is its main purpose evangelistic. The primary purpose of prophecy is to be found in Peter's statement about the use of our God given gifts. *"...so that in all things God may be glorified through Jesus Christ to whom belongs the glory..." (I Pet. 4:11).*

The fulfillment of predictive prophecy is proof that He (Yahweh) is God. (See I Sam. 12:22, 17:46, Josh. 3:10,

Ps. 106:8, Is. 41:22-23, 48:3-5, Ezek. 20:9). As He controls and brings to pass the things He predicts He proves Himself and is glorified as the only wise God (Rom. 16:27), the King eternal, immortal and invisible (I Tim. 1:17).

The Personal Purpose: To Purify Man

Prophecy is not given to increase our vain knowledge, but to improve our lives, to prepare us for the future and make us acceptable to God. Prophecy impels us to ask the probing question. *"Since all these things are to be...what sort of people ought you to be in holy conduct and godliness, looking for and hastening the coming of the day of God,..." (II Pet. 3:11-12).*

The answer is given in *Titus 2:12-13* *"...deny ungodliness and worldly desires and to live sensibly, righteously and godly in the present age, looking for the blessed hope and the appearing of the glory of our great God and Savior, Christ Jesus,..."*

The demonstration of a holy life is valid proof of the depth and sincerity of ones interest in prophecy. As the Apostle John wrote in *I John 3:3* *"Everyone who has this hope fixed on him purifies himself just as He is pure."*

Dr. J. Barton Payne wrote, "The entire course of history has been designed for the achievement of holiness."

The Practical Purpose:
To Enlighten and Encourage the Church

Prophecy is not written to and for the world. Prophecy is written to and for the church to promote faith and faithfulness in its continuing and consistent worship and ministry.

A Motivation for Worship Hebrews 10:19-39

As we see the day (of Christ's return) drawing near we are to increase our assembling together for Christian worship and fellowship. Our clamor for fewer and shorter worship services and sermons testifies to the insincerity and shallowness of our professed eager anticipation of our Lord's return. The purpose of our increased assemblies is not evangelism (the saving of the world), but edification (the building up of the Body of Christ). We are to encourage and stimulate each other to love one another, to exercise our ministries to one another and together to hold fast the confidence of our hope without wavering.

A Motivation for Ministry II Timothy 4:1-5
On the basis of the anticipated appearing of Jesus, Paul charges Timothy to *"...fulfill your ministry."* This is a good word to and for all Christians. We all have a ministry to fulfill. The fulfillment of prophecy and the anticipation of Christ's return should activate passive Christians. *"Therefore, gird your minds for action, keep sober in spirit, fix your hope completely on the grace to be brought to you at the revelation of Jesus Christ" (I Pet. 1:13).* Mark 13:34-36 reminds us that the expectation of our returning Master should be a wake-up call to each of us.

The Promissory Purpose: To Excite the Church

Prophecy is intended to give the church enough of a window into her glorious future so that she should be excited and eager to be faithful and to enter eventually into her inheritance. Peter assures us we have an inheritance (I Pet. 1:3-25). A will has been written by God and we are the named beneficiaries. We are chosen according to the foreknowledge of God and sprinkled with the blood of Christ so as to be born again to a living hope (inheritance). Being the children of God we are joint heirs with Christ of the estate of God (Rom. 8:17). Space will not permit us to give the specifics of our inheritance nor is that our purpose at this time. We want only to establish that one purpose of prophecy is to give us a preliminary reading of God's will which enumerates the riches of our promised inheritance.

Conclusion

Jesus had a twofold concern for the church in her pursuit of prophecy. He was concerned that she should not be deceived and misled (Mt. 24:4 & 11). Millions are being deceived and misled even by sincere and well-meaning pastors and teachers. One reason I concentrated on the study of Biblical prophecy in my latter years was to avoid being deceived and to deliver others from it. Deception is worse, in some ways, than persecution. Persecution comes from our enemies. Deception can come at the hands of our friends and well-intended persons who love us and share our faith in the Lord Jesus Christ.

Jesus' second concern was that the church shall not be afraid of the future (Mt. 24:6). Much prophetic teaching and preaching is geared to engender fear. This is especially true the way some teach the book of the Revelation. The general purpose of prophecy is to offer comfort not to instill panic or terror in the church. The blessed hope is too frequently portrayed as the bloody horror. Jesus said, *"When these things begin to take place, straighten up and lift up your heads because your redemption draws near" (Luke 21:28).*

M r. Kramer welcomes meaningful dialogue with anyone regarding what he has written.

Mr. Kramer also publishes an eight page Bible Study periodical in alternate months titled <u>Second Thoughts</u> which is available free of any costs to anyone who will provide a readable address.

Write:

Rev. Robert L. Kramer
42 Evans Avenue
Sinking Spring, PA 19608
Or call:
(610) 670-5108

CPSIA information can be obtained at www.ICGtesting.com
Printed in the USA
LVOW11s0916070914

402860LV00002B/232/P